1 Literature – Just Imagine …

1. Sighting a vampire

Bram Stoker's Dracula *(1897) is the most famous novel of the vampire genre and a model for the many films dealing with Count Dracula and vampires. The notorious Count Dracula contacts an English lawyer, Harker, who visits the count in his Transsylvanian Castle. There the lawyer experiences the most dreadful supernatural happenings. He records these in his diary. Some fragments of it are printed below, but they have become mixed up.*

1. Read each of the fragments carefully. Try to work out what is going on without knowing every word.
2. Underline those phrases which give you a clue as to the context of each fragment.
3. Number the fragments to show their correct order.

(7) When he left me I went to my room. After a little while, not hearing any sound, I came out and went up the stone stair to where I could look towards the south. There was some sense of freedom in the vast expanse, inaccessible though it was to me, as compared with the narrow darkness of the courtyard.

vast [ɑː] extremely large – **inaccessible** [ˌɪnækˈsesəbl] not able to be reached

( ) The window at which I stood was tall and deep, stone-mullioned, and though weather-worn, was still complete; but it was evidently many a day since the case had been there. I drew back behind the stonework, and looked carefully out. What I saw was the Count's head coming out from the window. I did not see the face, but I knew the man by the neck and the movement of his back and his arms. In any case, I could not mistake the hands which I had had so many opportunities of studying.

case here (l. 3): Fensterladen

( ) Looking out on this, I felt that I was indeed in prison, and I seemed to want a breath of fresh air, though it were of the night. I am beginning to feel this nocturnal existence tell on me. It is destroying my nerve. I start at my own shadow, and am full of all sorts of horrible imaginings. God knows that there is ground for any terrible fear in this accursed place! I looked out over the beautiful expanse, bathed in soft yellow moonlight till it was almost as light as day. In the soft light, the distant hills became melted, and the shadows in the valleys and gorges of velvety blackness.

nocturnal [nɒkˈtɜːnl] active at night – **accursed** [əˈkɜːsɪd] dreadful – **to melt** schmelzen – **gorge** deep, steep valley – **velvet** Samt

( ) I was at first interested and somewhat amused, for it is wonderful how small a matter will interest and amuse a man when he is a prisoner. But my very feelings changed to repulsion and terror when I saw the whole man slowly emerge from the window and begin to crawl down the castle wall over that dreadful abyss, *face down*, with his cloak spreading out around him like great wings.

repulsion [rɪˈpʌlʃn] feeling that s.th. is so awful it makes you sick – **cloak** coat without sleeves
abyss [əˈbɪs] very steep drop

( ) The mere beauty seemed to cheer me; there was peace and comfort in every breath I drew. As I leaned from the window my eye was caught by something moving a storey below me, and somewhat to the left, where I imagined, from the lie of the rooms, that the windows of the Count's own room would look out.

mere on its own

(6) At first I could not believe my eyes: I thought it was some trick of the moonlight, some weird effect of shadow; but I kept looking, and it could be no delusion. I saw the fingers and toes grasp the corners of the stones, worn clear of the mortar by the stress of years, and by thus using every projection and inequality move downwards with considerable speed, just as a lizard moves along a wall.

weird very strange – **delusion** illusion – **mortar** material between stones in stone walls – **projection** part sticking out – **lizard** ['--] Eidechse

Literature – Just Imagine ...

2. In a bank but not held up

1. *The following expressions are the main ones you will need in a bank. Look up the ones you do not know or cannot work out.*

   to exchange money – teller – bank manager – bank clerk – to withdraw money from an account – to pay by cheque – to fill in the amount in words and figures – to open a bank account – credit card – to write and sign a cheque – cheque card – service card – account holder – to pay by cheque – to cash a cheque – pay-in book – customer – cash dispenser – interest – to transfer money – to deposit money

2. *You are in London as an exchange student. A cousin of yours has just arrived in London for the start of a ten-month stay, though his/her English is poor. At a suburban branch of a bank, (s)he asks you to translate. Write in the translations, then act this out in groups of three.*

Bank clerk: Good morning. What can I do for you?

You: Sie möchte wissen, wie sie Dir behilflich sein kann.

Friend: Guten Tag. Ich möchte ein Konto eröffnen.

You: Good morning. My friend wants to open an account.

Bank clerk: I see. What kind of account?

You: Sie möchte wissen, _____

Friend: Ich weiß nicht – ich bin ab jetzt zehn Monate hier und bekomme regelmäßig Geld von meinen Eltern überwiesen.

You: _____

_____

Bank clerk: You need a savings account. How old are you? There is a special account for under-eighteens.

You: _____

_____

Friend: Ich bin gerade siebzehn geworden.

You: _____

Bank clerk: That's good. You can open a Young Person's Savings Account. It gives you 5% interest.

You: _____

_____

Friend: Gut. Und wie hebe ich Geld ab? Kann ich den Geldautomaten benutzen?

You: _____

Bank clerk: You withdraw money from the cash dispenser with a service card. It's easy to use. We send you a monthly magazine with tips and competitions, and you get a cash bonus when you open the account.

You: _____

Friend: Klingt gut!

You: _____

Bank clerk: O.K. then. Would you just like to fill in these forms, please, and sign them? We will also need proof of your present address, and a letter from your parents guaranteeing payment.

You: _____

_____

_____

Friend: Habe ich beides dabei.

You: _____

Bank clerk: Good! Well, it shouldn't take long now.

You: _____

Friend, you: Danke! / Thank you.

3. A picture can speak volumes

*Do **either** question 1 **or** question 2.*

1. a) *Look at picture A. What do you think is the connection between the woman and the girl? Where are they?*

   b) *Something has just happened. What?*

   c) *Invent the monologue that the girl is conducting in her head at this moment. What thoughts might she have about what has just happened? How is she feeling?*

   d) *Now imagine the two people speak to each other (e.g. the girl turns around when the woman says something to her). With a partner, invent the dialogue. You could even make it into a short piece of drama with suitable stage directions. Then act it out in class.*

2. a) *Picture B conveys an atmosphere but very little information. What might be the connection between the two people?*

   b) *How do you think the photographer created this effect?*

   c) *Describe what you can see.*

   d) *Describe what you cannot see, i.e. the room. Try to convey the atmosphere (e.g.: What is the light falling on? What is in shadow? What colours are there? Music?)*

A

B

Literature – Just Imagine ...

4. Not a minute to spare

The hero of Mark Twain's A Connecticut Yankee in King Arthur's Court *(1889), a New England factory worker in the 19th century, receives a blow over the head which sends him straight into King Arthur's early medieval world. There he is imprisoned and condemned to death. His only chance of survival is to think up some 19th-century trick that might impress the 6th-century royal court. He knows that the sun will be darkened for a time shortly before he is to die ...*

In translating literary texts it is important to copy the style as closely as possible without translating word for word. The following exercises take you step-by-step through such a translation:

1. *Draw a ring around the letter of the translation which in your opinion is most suitable. If you can think of something even more suitable, write it next to d.*

The door opened, and some men-at-arms appeared. The leader said: "The stake is ready. Come!" The stake! The strength went out of me, and I almost fell down. It is hard to get one's breath at such a time, such lumps come into one's throat, and such gaspings; but as soon as I could speak, I said: "But this is a mistake – the execution is tomorrow." "Order changed; been set forward a day. Haste thee!" I was lost. There was no help for me. I was dazed, stupefied; I had no command over myself; I only wandered purposely about, like one out of his mind ... [...]	Die Tür öffnete sich und einige Bewaffnete erschienen. Ihr Anführer sagte: „Der Scheiterhaufen ist bereit. Komm!" Der Scheiterhaufen! [1] , und ich [2] . Es ist schwer, in solch einem Augenblick weiterzuatmen, [3] und man nach Atem ringen muß. Aber sobald ich wieder sprechen konnte, sagte ich: „Aber das ist ein [4] , die Hinrichtung ist morgen." „Anweisung geändert; sie ist einen Tag vorverlegt worden. Beeile dich!" Ich war verloren. Es gab keine [5] für mich. Ich war benommen, betäubt; ich hatte keine Kontrolle mehr über mich; ich wanderte bloß ziellos auf und ab wie [6] [...]

1. a) Ich wurde schwach.
   b) Alle Kraft wich aus meinem Körper
   c) Ich fühlte mich kraftlos

   d) _____

2. a) fiel fast hin
   b) sank beinahe zu Boden
   c) wäre beinahe zu Boden gestürzt

   d) _____

3. a) wenn man so einen Kloß im Hals hat
   b) wenn es einem so die Kehle zuschnürt
   c) weil man einen Frosch im Hals hat

   d) _____

4. a) Fehler
   b) Versehen
   c) Irrtum

   d) _____

5. a) Hilfe
   b) Rettung
   c) Unterstützung

   d) _____

6. a) ein Wahnsinniger
   b) besessen
   c) ein Irrer

   d) _____

2. *Complete the translation of the next passage:*

As the soldiers assisted me across the court the stillness was so profound that if I had been blindfold I should have supposed I was in a solitude instead of walled in by four thousand people. There was not a movement perceptible in those masses of humanity; they were as rigid as stone images, and as pale; and dread sat upon every	Als die Soldaten mich über den Hof geleiteten, herrschte so tiefe Stille, daß ich – falls meine Augen verbunden gewesen wären – angenommen hätte, mich ¹_____ statt von 4000 Menschen ²_____ zu sein. Keine Bewegung war in der Menschenmenge wahrzunehmen, sie waren

Literature – Just Imagine ...

countenance. This hush continued while I was being chained to the stake...[...] Then there was a pause, and a deeper hush, if possible, and a man knelt down at my feet with a blazing torch ...	³_____ _____ und ⁴_____ _____, ⁵_____ zeigte sich in jedem Gesicht. Die Totenstille hielt an, während ich an den Pfahl gekettet wurde ... [...] Dann gab es eine Unterbrechung, ⁶_____ _____, wenn das überhaupt möglich war. Und ein Mann mit einer ⁷_____ Fackel kniete zu meinen Füßen nieder.

3. *Now for the climax.*
   a) When you first read the passage, try to work out the meaning of words you have not heard before from their contexts.
   b) Then underline these words and look at the definitions given below.
   c) Translate the whole passage. Make sure your style in German corresponds to that of the rest of the translation.

I waited two or three moments: then looked up; he was standing there petrified. With a common impulse the multitude rose slowly up and stared into the sky. I followed	their eyes; as sure as guns, there was my eclipse beginning! The life went boiling through my veins; I was a new man!

petrified so frightened that one cannot move – **multitude** large crowd – **eclipse** [-'-] *Sonnenfinsternis* – **vein** [veɪn] *Ader*

5. Autumn

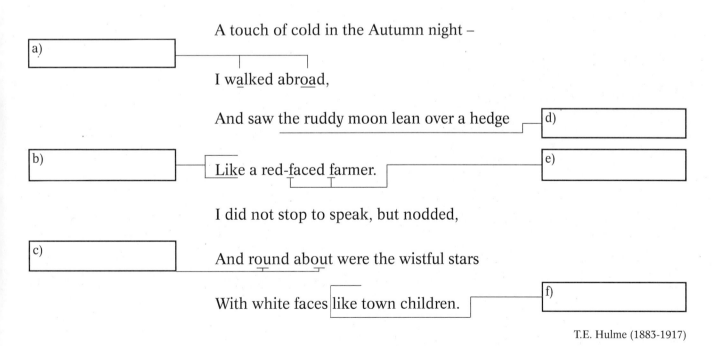

T.E. Hulme (1883-1917)

1. *Each of the boxes stands for a poetic device (see your textbook, pages 15–18) that is used in the poem. Fill in the boxes.*

5

Literature – Just Imagine …

2. Define devices d–f:

   d) _____

   e) _____

   f) _____

3. The word "ruddy" will probably be new to you (it is not used often in English), but you may have gained a sense of the meaning when reading the poem. Write down what you think it could mean, then look it up in a dictionary. Were you close?

   What you think the word means   **What the dictionary says**

   ruddy _____   _____

4. Now look up the word "wistful". Does it mean what you thought it did?
5. Underline the word(s) that best fit(s) the mood of the poem.

   melancholy   optimistic   peaceful   _____ (your suggestion)

6. The Little Old Lady and the law

Having stopped the underground train, the Little Old Lady was charged £100 by London Transport for causing unnecessary delay. As a result she took the Unpleasant Man to court. Tracy was asked to act as a witness.

Put in connecting words or phrases from the list below to complete Tracy's statement. Use each of the words and phrases at least once.

> so, but, however, finally, after a while, because, when, as soon as, then, and, even though

On 15th October at about midday, Sam – that's my neighbour – and I took the Tube to Charing Cross. On the way I tested Sam's knowledge of geography _____ it looked like he was going to fail his geography exam. An old lady got on at Kennington. _____ she heard us, she joined in _____ answered some questions herself. _____ a man got in. He looked very unfriendly _____ started smoking _____ it was not allowed. We all looked at him, _____ nobody dared say anything. _____ the old lady asked him to stop smoking, he ignored her, _____ she kept on complaining. _____ he challenged her to take the cigarette out of his mouth herself, _____ she didn't move. The atmosphere became more tense _____ he lit up a second cigarette. _____ the old lady threatened to pull the emergency chain. The other passengers didn't want a delay or an accident, _____ they tried to stop her. She didn't listen, _____ . You know the rest.

Literature – Just Imagine ...

7. Words? What words?

The box contains many of the terms you have learned for talking about literature. How many can you find? The letters are always in a straight line but can go in any direction. Read the clues below first and try to work out what the words are (the glossary of literary terms in your textbook will help you). Then look for them in the box. Using a pencil, draw a ring around each word you find.

```
M E S H O R T S T O R Y A
D O R U P A L A I R P E L
A R H O Z O D T I M T N L
Y O A N T I T H E S I S I
S P A M P H R T I A R L T
N T N I A L E N Y N R T E
S D S N E Q O M N E H O R
O L I O C G U T M I Y R A
S L I R A T S Y I P T O T
O M E T A P H O R O H D I
R E O V A R I A O I M U O
H R U N O N L I N E N N N
P K T U V N P O Y K T A A
```

1. The most important character in a story — *protagonist*
2. *Robinson Crusoe* is one _____
3. War and peace, old and young _____
4. My love is a rose _____
5. Action performed on a stage _____
6. The storyline of a piece of narrative writing _____
7. Saying s.th. and expressing the opposite _____
8. My love is like a rose ... _____
9. Part of a poem _____
10. Tall trees, surprising stories _____
11. Enjambement _____
12. The regular pattern of stresses in a poem _____
13. Relatively short fictional prose text _____
14. Characters who receive little attention _____
15. Pattern made when two stressed syllables sound the same _____

Literature – Just Imagine …

The big city and you

The billboard is all yours.
Write a poem entitled "The Big City and Me". Your poem should have exactly eleven words. It can rhyme, it can be free verse or it can be concrete poetry. And it's just for you. (If you want to, of course, you can show it to your neighbour or someone else.)

2 Environmentally Yours

1. Test your vocabulary about the environment

1. Combine the words on the left and the words on the right: you will find 21 expressions that have something to do with the environment, and how to protect it.

(D)

1. acid	• bank	1. *saurer Regen*
2. bottle	• bottle	2. _____
3. carbon	• cancer	3. _____
4. catalytic	• converter	4. _____
5. endangered	• dioxide	5. _____
6. environmentally	• disposal	6. _____
7. fossil	• effect	7. _____
8. global	• farming	8. _____
9. greenhouse	• food	9. _____
10. health	• forest	10. _____
11. landfill	• friendly	11. _____
12. nuclear	• fuel	12. _____
13. organic	• layer	13. _____
14. ozone	• petrol	14. _____
15. rain	• powder	15. _____
16. renewable	• power	16. _____
17. returnable	• rain	17. _____
18. skin	• site	18. _____
19. unleaded	• sources of energy	19. _____
20. washing	• species	20. _____
21. waste	• warming	21. _____

2. Now translate the expressions into German but be careful not to translate them word for word.

Environmentally Yours

2. What do *you* use?

These are some electrical appliances you probably have in your household. Fill in the boxes after reading the clues to find out the question you should keep asking yourself. If you're not sure what the electrical appliance is called in English, use a dictionary.

1. You heat your meal with it very quickly
2. Your shirt looks wonderful when you have used this
3. Do you really want to watch another film?
4. Do you have to clean your teeth with an electric one?
5. Are you too lazy to wash your plates yourself?
6. Part of a hi-fi system that you put cassettes into
7. You use it after you have washed your hair
8. You cut your beard with it
9. You clean your carpet with it
10. You use it to show someone your holiday photos
11. You use this to speak to your friends who are not around
12. It keeps your food fresh
13. It helps you with your work, and perhaps you play games on it, too
14. It keeps your food fresh even longer
15. It takes messages for you when you are not at home
16. You watch it
17. You cut the grass in your garden with it
18. Part of your stereo which causes the sound to become louder
19. You use it after washing your clothes

3. What would happen if ...?

1. *Imagine what would happen if we didn't bother about our environment. Write complete conditional sentences, using different verbs each time.*

a) If we all used public transport instead of cars, _____

b) _____ if we only used oil and coal for energy.

c) Our forests would disappear if _____

d) If _____

2. *Now imagine what your life would have been like if you had lived 200 years ago. The list of appliances in exercise 2 will give you some ideas of things that did not exist then. Vary your sentences as much as possible.*

a) If I had lived 200 years ago, _____

_____

b) _____

  if _____

c) _____

_____

3. *What will life on earth be like in the 21st century? Think of what activities, laws, and ways of thinking will have to be changed, if our planet is to be saved.*

a) If we do not _____

_____

b) _____

  if _____

c) _____

_____

4. National park

1. Read the box on "pun" on page 49 of your textbook.
2. Now describe the pun in the cartoon – what is the cartoonist making fun of?

5. Everything looks clean and bright!

A new nuclear power station is going to be opened soon. Mrs Jackson, a reporter for the local newspaper, interviews one of the engineers, Mr Franklin:

Reporter: Everything looks perfectly clean and bright. When will the power station go into operation?
Franklin: In three weeks. And it will remain clean, and it will not harm our environment either!
Reporter: You may be right, unless you have an accident.
Franklin: The chances of an accident are extremely small. All the systems are fail safe. If one single mistake is made, the reactor will shut down automatically, and it can't be switched on again without a full investigation.
Reporter: Didn't they have fail safe systems in Chernobyl, too?

Environmentally Yours

Franklin: The kind of accident that happened in Chernobyl simply can't happen in this country. You can take my word for that. The risks have been reduced to vanishing point.
Reporter: But a catastrophe is possible if, for example, an engineer goes mad and throws all the wrong switches.
Franklin: There will never be fewer than three on duty in the control room at any time. The other two will be able to override anything the other one does. We have thought of everything, I can assure you.

After the power station has been opened, Mrs Jackson tells one of her colleagues about the interview. Fill in the gaps in reported speech (cf Klett Grundgrammatik *§ 150-153).*

Well, I opened the interview saying how perfectly clean and bright everything looked, and I then asked when _____

Mr Franklin told me _____

and then he added _____

I answered _____

But Mr Franklin explained _____

_____

_____

When I asked him _____

he said _____

_____. I still wasn't satisfied and said _____

_____. But Mr Franklin told me _____

_____

_____

He was absolutely certain _____

6. A History of WWF

Read this text and fill in the gaps with the verbs in brackets, using the correct tense and either the active or the passive voice. In some cases, you may need to add a modal verb like "would". Before you begin, underline all the words or phrases in the text which point to which tense should be used.

In just over three decades, WWF (to become) _____ one of the world's largest and most respected private international conservation organizations,

Environmentally Yours

with supporters distributed throughout five continents. To date, WWF (to invest) _____ over US$ 525 million in more than 11,000 projects in 130 countries.

One of the most important figures in WWF's early history (to be) _____ the renowned* British biologist, Sir Julian Huxley. The first Director General of UNESCO, Huxley (to help, also) _____ found a scientific conservation institution, now known as IUCN – The World Conservation Union. In 1960, Huxley (to go) _____ to East Africa to advise UNESCO on wildlife conservation in the area. He (to be) _____ shocked at what he (to see) _____. On his return to London, he (to write) _____ three articles for the *Observer* newspaper in which he (to warn) _____ the British public that habitat* (to destroy) _____ and animals (to hunt) _____ at such a rate that much of the region's wildlife (to disappear) _____ within the next 20 years. Huxley (to receive) _____ many letters. So he (to ask) _____ Max Nicholson to form an international organization to raise funds* for international conservation. By spring 1961, Nicholson (to gather) _____ together a group of scientists and other experts. The group (to decide) _____ to base its operations in neutral Switzerland, where IUCN (to transfer, already) _____ its headquarters to a villa on the northern shores of Lake Geneva. The new organization, which (to plan) _____ to work closely with IUCN, (to be) _____ to share this villa.

Meanwhile, Chi-Chi the panda (to arrive) _____ at London Zoo. Aware of the need for a strong, recognizable symbol that (to overcome) _____ all language barriers, the group (to agree) _____ that the big furry animal (to make) _____ an excellent logo. The black and white panda (to come, since) _____ to stand as a symbol for the conservation movement as a whole. WWF (to form, officially) _____ and (to register) _____ as a charity on 11 September 1961.

The founders (to decide) _____ that the most efficient approach (to be) _____ to set up offices in different countries. The first national appeal*, with HRH The Duke of Edinburgh as President, (to launch*) _____ in the United Kingdom on 23 November, 1961. On 1 December it (to follow) _____ by the United States, and a few days later, Switzerland. Since then, WWF (to grow, considerably) _____.

Abridged from *A History of WWF* by WWF-World Wide Fund For Nature, 1994. © WWF-World Wide Fund For Nature (formerly World Wildlife Fund).

renowned well-known – **habitat** natural environment in which an animal usually lives – **to raise funds** to find money – **appeal** request for money and help – **to launch** *here:* to start, to begin

Environmentally Yours

7. Radiation around us

The following text appeared in a brochure about radiation. Translate it into German, trying to keep to the style of the English text. Avoid translating certain structures and phrases too literally – try to find good German equivalents.

> Radiation has become of concern to us all. But there is nothing new about radiation. Although it was discovered less than a century ago, we have lived with it since the beginning of time. However hard we try, we cannot avoid it. Natural radiation comes from four sources: outer space, the earth itself, the air we breathe, and all our food and drink. In addition, we use radiation in medicine, manufacturing industry, agriculture, pollution control, research, and in the production of energy in nuclear power stations.

Just for you

Some people get everything wrong! Having read and discussed the texts in the chapter "Environmentally Yours", the students had to write down what they knew about the following:

Al Gore • Chris Rea • Chief Seattle • Mahatma Gandhi • Holden • Ecotopia • Hunterston • WWF • the Mississippi • the Exxon Valdez • the Braer

Here are some of the answers that were given:

- Al Gore was a friend of Mahatma Gandhi's; he wrote anecdotes about him.
- Chief Seattle was called the Father of all Waters.
- Holden is an Australian singer.
- Chris Rea is president of WWF.
- Hunterston is the capital of Ecotopia.
- The Exxon Valdez sank in the Mississippi.
- The Braer is a nuclear power station near Glasgow.

What would you have written?

3 Welcome to Europe

1. Three different ways of advertising the same thing

1. *Most people have at some time or other come across stereotypes about people from different countries. Look at the following ads. Then complete the sentences, saying what they imply about each individual country and its inhabitants.*

a) Her Gracious Majesty's Hammer indicates _____

_____

_____

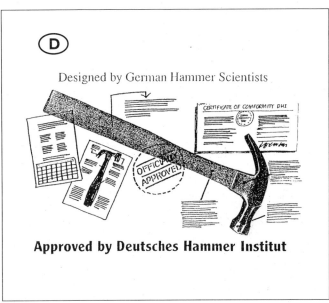

b) The German Hammer symbolizes _____

_____

_____

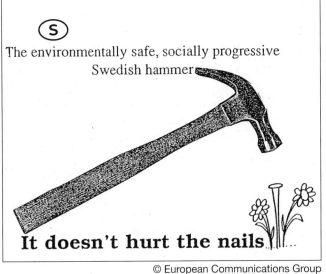

c) The Swedish Hammer suggests _____

_____

_____

2. *Try to design a similar ad for a European hammer.*

Welcome to Europe

3. "dis-, il-, ir-, un-, in-, im-" are prefixes used at the beginning of verbs, adjectives, adverbs and nouns in order to form words that have the opposite meaning, e.g.

   safe   <u>unsafe</u>

a) Look at the following words and write down the prefix which goes with each of them.

to agree	_____	responsible	_____
regular	_____	possible	_____
polite	_____	correct	_____
able	_____	relevant	_____
employment	_____	equal	_____
legal	_____	logical	_____
honest	_____	to like	_____
dependence	_____		

b) Can you think of any other opposites formed in the same way?

4. What they said in Parliament.

Fill in the gaps in the sentences below. Use words from your list of opposites (3).

E.g. We have to do something about <u>unemployment</u> in Europe. (the number of people who do not have jobs)

1. What he has just said seems to us _____. (of no importance)

2. The Prime Minister was (not rational) _____ in his argumentation.

3. My political friends and I _____. (are not of the same opinion)

4. This procedure is _____. (against the law)

5. We want to keep our country's _____. (sovereignty)

6. I _____ (am not pleased with) what some bureaucrats in Brussels do.

7. I think they are _____. (not aware of the consequences of what they are doing)

2. Unification – union – unison – unit – unity

Using a dictionary, put the correct word (unification – union – unison – unit – unity) into the gaps.

E.g. They are working for the <u>union</u> of the two countries.

1. A number of European states form a _____.

2. Europe must speak in _____ on matters of foreign policy.

3. German _____ happened in 1990.

4. There should be greater _____ in the party.

5. The family is the basic _____ of our society.

6. One of the goals in Europe is monetary _____.

Welcome to Europe

7. The monetary _____ of Europe is the ECU.
8. The _____ of the Soviet Socialist Republics does not exist any more.
9. A process of economic _____ is taking place in Europe.
10. For a long time German _____ seemed impossible.
11. The member states do not always act in _____.
12. There was no _____ among the delegates of the conference.

3. Capitals of Europe

24 European capitals (English names) are hidden in this network of letters. The letters of their names run either from left to right, from right to left, from top to bottom, bottom to top, or diagonally. Letters may also overlap. Two examples are given. Find the remaining 22 capitals. To help you, the first letters of the capitals are in alphabetical order.

```
U M O S C O W T Z A I G R Q W
S I R A P T S D I R D A M S T
S E J H D A T H E N S A C T M
B Q U L F N R H C E D T S A O
I Z P L H N F S H R V E L K N
R W E V C E U S E W P D L G I
N B E R L I N T L A R U E P L
A X L O E V S X D I X G B U B
N V U N F M V U B E A M R T U
I E K Y A U B T M T F W U Z D
K D G I T J Z B A N O L S O R
N E H A G M O C E I P R S I W
I P A S H U L I M W F N E B A
S R D S R N H N O D N O L E R
L A R G Y O E K R S D B S R S
E G T C O B J P A P Y S U N A
H U S T O C K H O L M I T E W
W E B A N K A R A C U L I D R
```

A _____
A _____
A _____
B _____
B _____
B _____
B _____
B _____
C _____
D _____
H _____
L Luxembourg
L _____
L _____
M _____
M _____
O _____
P _____
P _____
R _____
S _____
S _____
V Vienna
W _____

Welcome to Europe

4. Which preposition?

to agree, to apply, to look, to talk   ▸   with at on to for after upon about

Fill in the gaps in the sentences below using the prepositions given.
E.g. The Six didn't agree <u>about</u> Britain joining the EC.

1. Britain applied _____ full membership of the EC for the first time in 1963.

2. Many British people looked _____ the EC as a chance to improve their economic situation.

3. The member states couldn't agree _____ a common policy towards Britain.

4. In 1967 Britain again applied _____ the EC to be admitted.

5. Germany didn't agree _____ President de Gaulle when he vetoed Britain's becoming a full member of the EC.

6. The British government applied _____ Parliament for approval before becoming a full member of the EC.

7. The Prime Minister had to talk _____ a number of MPs who opposed Britain's application in order to change their minds.

8. Several MPs insisted that the Prime Minister should concentrate on looking _____ British interests.

9. Finally France agreed _____ Britain joining the EC.

10. Before Britain was admitted the terms of her entry had to be talked _____.

11. The British negotiators looked _____ the treaty very carefully. They were looking _____ ways to modify the conditions of entry.

5. It's Euro-time!

1. Since the 1960s words beginning with "Euro-" have become fashionable. Combine the words on the left with the correct definitions.

1. Eurocrat   •   a) Inability of EU countries to cope with the commercial challenges of new technology
2. Euromania   •   b) Extreme dislike or fear of the EU
3. Eurostar   •   c) Story about EU rules or regulations that frightens people
4. Eurosclerosis   •   d) Packaging produced to EU standards
5. Eurobabble   •   e) Train that runs through the Tunnel connecting London and Paris
6. Euroscare   •   f) Extreme excitement over Europe
7. Europhobia   •   g) False story about EU regulations
8. Europack   •   h) Member of the administration of the EU
9. Euromyth   •   i) The jargon of EU documents and regulations

2. Write a definition for each of the following "Euro-words".

1. Euro-MP _____

2. Europop _____

Welcome to Europe

3. Eurosceptic _____

4. Euro-summit _____

3. Invent three more "Euro-words". Give them to your partner and tell him or her to write a definition for each one.

6. The curved cucumber

The following press item was found in a British quality paper.

Farmers and greengrocers will have to grapple* with yet another of the increasingly more numerous EU regulations. As straight or only slightly curved cucumbers are easier to pack and less likely to break or bruise when stored and transported, they will in future enjoy class I status according to EU quality standards. Curved cucumbers will be classified as a class II product and as a consequence will fetch a lower price.

to grapple with to try hard to solve s.th.

Imagine you are a reporter for a popular paper. Rewrite this news item in the way a popular paper would do so. Remember that tabloids exaggerate and distort facts. Here are some words and phrases that might help you:

to go mad over s.th. – an absurd/ a crazy/ grotesque idea/ act/ measure – to be angry – to fly into a rage/ to see red/ to explode – to make one's blood boil – to complain/ to scold/ to curse – to hatch up next/ to be up to next – not to put up with/ not to take it/ not to hold still/ not to swallow it

How silly can you get?

_____

_____

_____

_____

_____

The Guardian, 21 March 1992

Invent a caption for the last speech bubble.

Welcome to Europe

7. An interview with a Euro-MP

A prominent Euro-MP gave a reporter the following interview:

R: How have developments in Central and Eastern Europe since the end of the Cold War affected the EU in your opinion?
MP: The dramatic changes in Central and Eastern Europe have created what is perhaps the greatest challenge for the EU so far. Suddenly 400 million people, who have shaken off communism, are waiting at the doors of the EU wanting to be allowed in.
R: How is Western Europe to meet this challenge?
MP: The question is whether the West will open its borders for trade and economic cooperation. Will it admit countries like Hungary, Poland, the Czech Republic in a few years or will it lock them out?
R: Won't it be far too expensive to extend the Union in this way?
MP: Taking in countries like Greece and Portugal was expensive, too. I am convinced that in the long run both sides will come out winners.
R: How is that going to happen?
MP: The West must focus on high technology, capital-intensive production and the East must take care of labour-intensive, low-capital production. Trade is not a one-sided thing. If the East can export to the West, it can also import from the West. And this will make Europe as a whole more competitive.
R: Thank you very much for this interview.

The newspaper did not publish what the Euro-MP said in the form of an interview but as a newspaper report. Complete the report using reported speech (cf. Klett Grundgrammatik *§150–153). Try to find different ways of beginning the sentences so that they do not all begin in the same way. Choose from:*

> to add, to explain, to go on to say, to make it clear, to point out, to say, to wonder

When asked by our reporter about how the development in Central and Eastern Europe since the end of the Cold War had affected the EU, a prominent Euro-MP said _____

_____

_____

_____

_____

He pointed out that taking in countries like Greece and Portugal had been expensive, too. He made it clear that _____

_____

_____

_____

_____

_____

8. Never will Britain be the same again ...

The above phrase could have been written like this: Britain will never be the same again ... When used with special emphasis, negative or restrictive adverbials such as 'never', 'not only', 'hardly ... when', etc. are placed at the beginning of a sentence. In this case, inversion is necessary (see Klett Grundgrammatik § 149).

1. Rewrite the following sentences by changing the word order.

a) Not only is the Channel a geophysical barrier between Britain and France but it is also a psychological one.

   The Channel _____

b) Not until the end of the last century did swimming in the Channel arouse public interest.

   Swimming the Channel _____

c) Hardly had the South Eastern Railway Company started work on a twin tunnel in 1880 when the project was once again abandoned.

   The South Eastern Railway Company _____

d) No sooner had military strategists heard about the project than they began to oppose it.

   Military strategists _____

e) Seldom has a project caused as much controversy as the Tunnel.

   A project _____

2. Now complete the following sentences, starting with a negative or restrictive adverbial.

a) I have rarely welcomed anything with such enthusiasm.

   Rarely _____

b) I will never again travel by ferry; I have always disliked ferries.

   Never again _____

c) I not only think the Tunnel will make it easier for rabies* to reach Britain, but I also believe the new transport system will destroy the countryside.

   Not only _____

d) I wouldn't under any circumstances get into a train that runs under the sea.

   Under no circumstances _____

e) Business and industry have never before had the opportunities that the Tunnel now provides.

   Never before _____

rabies *Tollwut*

Welcome to Europe

9. Boom and gloom*

1. Fill in the gaps in this text using the prepositions given below. They may be used more than once.

| behind | to | over | since | through | between | by | from | towards | into | for |
| past | about | | of | out of | | | | | | |

150 years ago a railway line was built _____ London and Folkestone, and the little village was transformed _____ a major resort*. Magnificent houses and grand hotels, often with large parks, were built, which turned the place _____ a fashionable holiday destination _____ the upper circles of London's Victorian society.

Later Folkestone benefited _____ the ferry industry, which _____ many years created jobs and brought prosperity* _____ the town.

_____ the construction of the Tunnel people have started to worry _____ the future. Their town lies less than a kilometre southwest _____ the tunnel mouth, but _____ the busy construction site and Folkestone rises Castle Hill, which protects the town _____ the busy terminal. There are no road signs directing visitors _____ the town and once the cars leave the shuttle carriages they head straight _____ the motorway _____ London. The people in Folkestone are afraid _____ being left _____ by a scheme that gave them so much hope and reason _____ optimism. _____ the time they are _____ the Tunnel passengers will already have gone _____ the town; cafés, pubs, hotels and shops will be put _____ business. People are disgusted* and a feeling of gloom has settled _____ the town.

gloom feeling of sadness and hopelessness – **resort** popular holiday centre – **prosperity** state of being successful and rich – **disgusted** feeling a strong dislike for s.th.

2. Find words in the passage which mean the opposite of the following:

deserted   *busy*

out-of-date   _____

pessimism   _____

to feel secure   _____

simple   _____

pleased   _____

lower   _____

more   _____

poverty   _____

fearless   _____

to make a detour   _____

to destroy jobs   _____

to despair   _____

minor   _____

22

How European are you?

1. Is the Single Market
   a) a marriage bureau?
   b) a way of selling goods and services in Europe?
   c) the promotion company behind the Eurovision song contest?
   d) the opposite of a supermarket?

2. Is the EU
   a) Steven Spielberg's latest film about an extraterrestrial being?
   b) a political party?
   c) short for European Union?
   d) short for the standard-size European umbrella?

3. Did Britain join the EEC in
   a) 1939 (to form an alliance with France against Germany)?
   b) 1951 (due to the decline of the British Empire)?
   c) 1961 (at President de Gaulle's invitation)?
   d) 1973 (in order not to miss the boat)?

4. Is 1993
   a) a recently-discovered novel by George Orwell?
   b) a new telephone code for London?
   c) a heavy-metal rock band from Newcastle?
   d) when trade barriers fell all over Europe?

5. Is Brussels
   a) the capital of Belgium and seat of the EU Commission?
   b) a night club founded by Bertrand Russell?
   c) the plural of Brussel?
   d) a fruit or a vegetable?

6. Is the seat of the European Parliament
   a) on the Isle of Man?
   b) in Frankfurt?
   c) in Strasbourg?
   d) in Rome?

7. Was the Treaty of Accession
   a) the treaty through which Britain was admitted to the EEC?
   b) the treaty which guaranteed the existence of the British monarchy?
   c) the treaty that gave Greece, Portugal and Spain EEC status?
   d) an agreement about a common agricultural policy?

8. Is Maastricht
   a) a city in Holland?
   b) the Dutch word for mustard?
   c) where the EuroTunnel ends on the continent?
   d) the summer seat of the Dutch King?

9. Is ECU
   a) a popular disco in Paris?
   b) a newly developed electric car?
   c) a European exchange student programme?
   d) short for European Currency Unit?

10. Is Europe Day on
    a) January 1st (when the Treaty of Rome came into force in 1958)?
    b) May 9th (Robert Schuman's date of birth)?
    c) July 1st (when the Single European Act came into force in 1987)?
    d) November 9th (when the Berlin Wall collapsed in 1989)?

Choose the correct answer to each question to find out how European you are.

Solution: 1b; 2c; 3d; 4d; 5a; 6c; 7a; 8a; 9d; 10b.

Scores

If you have scored 17 – 20 points, you are a true European.
If you have totalled 15 – 16 points, you are not too sure of the facts, but you show an interest in European affairs.
If you have got 13 – 14 points, you are not well-informed. Read more newspapers!
A score of 10 – 12 points makes it obvious that you don't look far beyond your national borders.
If you have no more than 8 – 9 points, you still have a long way to go.
With fewer than 8 points you are slightly disoriented as far as Europe is concerned.

4 What is Culture Anyway?

1. Colours

1. Colours affect the atmosphere of a painting (see pages 8, 60 and 62 of your textbook). Look up any of the words on the palette you do not know in a dictionary.
2. Look at Edward Hopper's painting "Early Sunday Morning" on page 9 of your textbook. Making use of the colour adjectives on the palette, describe the colours used to create the quiet early morning atmosphere. Write four sentences describing different parts of the picture. The words below will help you – if you don't know their meaning, look them up in a dictionary. Try to vary your sentences.

| window-sill | curtain / blind | barber's pole | awning round the shop window | sky |
| upper storey / floor | pavement | fire hydrant | row of houses | shadow |

E.g. The walls of the upper storey of the row of houses are muted brown.

a) _____

b) _____

c) _____

d) _____

3. Now describe the colours of Hopper's painting again but this time, imagine that it is midday and that the sun is high in the sky. Some of the following words might help you, as well as the vocabulary from exercise 1:

to contrast with s.th. – to be in (stark) contrast to s.th. – to stand out – to be in harmony with s.th.

1. _____
2. _____
3. _____
4. _____
5. The colours in the painting at midday are _____ so the atmosphere is more _____.

What is Culture Anyway?

4. There are many expressions in English which include colours. Fill in the spaces in the following list. If you do not know an expression, think of what associations you have with certain colours, as this will help you.

Phrase with colour **Explanation**

1. to be in the red a) _____

2. in _____ b) written and not just spoken *(2 colours)*

3. to feel _____ c) to feel low and depressed

4. to give s.o. the green light d) _____

5. out of the _____ e) completely unexpectedly

6. to tell a white lie f) _____

7. to have green fingers g) _____

8. to be caught red-handed h) _____

9. the yellow pages i) _____

10. to be _____ j) to be covered with bruises *(2 colours)*

11. a black eye k) _____

2. Talking about the past

1. In "The fortieth anniversary" on page 64 of your textbook, two tenses are often used. Pick out all the (finite) verbs used in ll. 1–19. Name the two tenses used and quote an example of each. Say why each is used.

2. Now look at lines 20– 27. What two tenses are used here, and why?

3. Fill in the blanks in the following story, putting the verbs in brackets in the right tense. (You might need to use the passive in some cases.)

It's always the same old story: every time my father (to start) _____ a sentence with, "When I (to be) _____ a boy …" I (to know) _____ to expect trouble. According to him, back in the good old days, youngsters (to not spend) _____ all their money on trash, (to not leave) _____ the house without saying where they (to go) _____, (to answer back, never) _____ and so on, and so on. I (to sit back, usually, just) _____, (to try) _____ to think of something pleasant and (to not listen really) _____ to what he (to say) _____.

However, since yesterday evening I (to begin) _____ to realize that even my father (may be) _____ young once, perhaps. Here (to be) _____ what (to happen) _____. I (to buy, just) _____ a new CD with old recordings of The Beatles and (to disappear) _____ as usual into my room to play it at full blast*, like I (to do, always)

25

What is Culture Anyway?

_____, as I (to want) _____ to feel the beat. I (to settle down, hardly) _____ on my bed when my father (to burst) _____ into my room, without knocking, which (to be) _____ a custom of his I (to try) _____ to break for years, and (to say) _____, "When I (to be) _____ a boy ..." He (to look) _____ angry, or at least, very red in the face, so I (to take) _____ a deep breath and (to wait) _____ for the usual blah blah. But imagine my surprise when he (to finish off) _____ his sentence with "... we (to be into*) _____ the Beatles, too". He (to tell) _____ me about John Lennon, who (to shoot) _____ by a madman in 1980, and then (to go on) _____ to say, "I (to like) _____ Ringo Starr the most – nobody (to play) _____ the drums like Ringo, you (to know) _____. The Mersey Beat*, you (to not get) _____ anything like that nowadays. Anyone (to tell, ever) _____ you the Beatles (to put) _____ on the Honours List* in 1965? I (to wish) _____ you (to be able) _____ to see them – they (to be, really) _____ something. When I (to be) _____ a boy, we knew what we (to want) _____ and (to go out) _____ and (to do) _____ things, no matter what our parents (to say) _____. You (should see) _____ my Beatles haircut! It (to look) _____ terrific!"

It just goes to show: you never can tell, can you?

at full blast at full volume – **to be into s.th.** *(informal)* abfahren auf etwas – **Mersey Beat** characteristic pop music of the Beatles and other Liverpool groups in the 1960s – **Honours List** – list of people who have or are having an honour *(Titel)* given to them by the Queen (or King)

2. *In the instructions to the above text "right" means correct, but it can also mean "the opposite of left". Words like this, which are spelt alike but have different meanings are called homonyms. The following words occur in the text in one meaning. Each of them has at least one other meaning. Write a sentence using each of them, making this other meaning clear. If necessary, look up the words in a dictionary.*

	second meaning	example
e.g. right	<u>opposite of left</u>	<u>In Germany, cars drive on the right.</u>
sentence	_____	_____
back	_____	_____
just	_____	_____
even	_____	_____
beat	_____	_____
youth	_____	_____
matter	_____	_____

What is Culture Anyway?

3. Beauty and ugliness

1. Read through the text on page 67 of your textbook. Write down all the adjectives
   – with positive meanings which the two girls use to characterize themselves and their ideas
   – which have negative connotations or denotations (cf. box on page 114) and express how ugly the girls think modern architecture is.

beautiful/positive	ugly/negative

2. What other adjectives could you use to describe modern architecture?

_____

_____

_____

3. In lines 48–58 and 63–65, Lotte pretends she is showing a group of tourists around Computex House in London and does this in a very ironic way. Imagine you are now giving a group of people a guided tour of the Sydney Opera House (see page 66 of your textbook). Fill in the gaps in the following passage, making your text as dramatic as possible by including some of the adjectives from the lists above. The useful phrases for "Talking about architecture" on page 66 will help you, as well as the following words:

base – tourist attraction – curve – design – roof – contemporary – line

You are standing in front of the _____ Sydney Opera House, probably the best known _____ outside Australia, _____ in the years 1965–1973. It has two parts: the straight, solid _____ and the elegantly curved _____. Observe the _____, _____, _____ which make it one of the _____ examples of modern architecture in the world. The obvious intention of this _____ is to resemble as much as possible a(n) _____. Note the _____ on which it has been built, namely Sydney Harbour. The _____ responsible, Jørn Utzon, has made a(n) _____ contribution to _____ architecture.

27

What is Culture Anyway?

4. The Scream

1. Two friends are visiting the National Gallery in Oslo and are looking at Edvard Munch's painting The Scream *(before it was stolen!). You'll find a reproduction of it on page 60 of your textbook.*
When you read the following dialogue, you will see that the stage directions describing the emotions and reactions of the speakers are missing.
a) After reading each sentence, choose a suitable adjective from the list below which describes the character's feelings or reaction. (You may also use an adjective of your own choice which is not in the list.)

| amused | anxious | impatient | unmoved | excited | casual | nervous | embarrassed |
| angry | moved | aggressive | surprised | ironic | interested | curious | |

b) Then choose an introductory present participle from the list below to combine with the adjective. However, be careful – some of these participles are followed by an adverb or an adverbial phrase, not an adjective, so you might have to change your adjective into an adverb or use an adverbial phrase.

| seeming | growing | remaining | reacting | speaking | answering | getting |
| becoming | appearing | asking | whispering | | | |

Martin (*getting excited*) Hey come over here. Look what I've found! Have you ever seen anything like this before?

Michael (_____) Why are you talking so loudly? Everybody is looking at us.

Martin (_____) Well it's because it's such a weird picture. It makes my blood run cold.

Michael (_____) Really? It looks pretty normal to me.

Martin (_____) Normal? Oh come on! Take a good look at it. Look at the figure in the foreground.

Michael (_____) What about it?

Martin (_____) What do you mean: "What about it?" Look at it you silly fool.

(_____) It's frightening. It hasn't got a proper body, the head looks like a skull and it's terrified of something.

Michael (_____) Hey, you're right!

(_____) What's the picture called anyway?

(He leans over the safety barrier to get a better look at the title. The alarm goes off. Michael screams. Two attendants rush up and show them out.)

While being led out of the gallery

Martin (_____) Do you know what the picture's called?

Michael No, tell me.

Martin (_____) The picture's called "The Scream"!

What is Culture Anyway?

2. *Make a recording of the dialogue with a partner. Speak it as dramatically as possible.*

3. *Rewrite the following sentences, reporting on the dialogue "The Scream" by inserting the adjectives and adverbs which are in the brackets at the end of each sentence in the correct form (i.e. some of the adjectives will have to be put into adverb form). In some cases they can be inserted in more than one place, so you will have to choose the most suitable position, e.g.*

1. When Martin and Michael were visiting the National Gallery in Oslo, Martin grew excited and asked Michael if he had seen anything like Edvard Munch's "The Scream".
   (ever, sudden, very, before)

   When Martin and Michael were visiting the National Gallery in Oslo, Martin <u>suddenly</u> grew <u>very</u> excited and asked Michael if he had <u>ever</u> seen anything like Edvard Munch's "The Scream" <u>before</u>.

2. As Michael had not seen the picture he reacted angrily and asked Martin why he was talking.
   (yet, quite, extreme, impatient, so, loud)

3. When Michael looked at the picture he remained cool and did not appear impressed.
   (first, immediate, fairly, quick, very)

4. After Michael had had a look at the picture he reacted strongly and said he could understand why Martin had been moved.
   (extreme, good, very, now, so, good)

5. While the boys were being led out of the gallery, Michael was amused and asked Martin if he knew what the picture was called.
   (hurried, final, strange, rather, ironical)

"I tell you, Herb, forty-nine people can't be wrong!"
London Opinion, Jan. 1953 (Bruce Cavalier)

Why are these people standing on their heads?

What is Culture Anyway?

5. Acting is an exciting career

1. Read the statements below and decide to what extent you agree with them or not using the following scale: 0 (total disagreement) to 6 (total agreement). Put a cross on each line in the diagram where appropriate. You will need to refer to "Living dozens of great lives" on page 70 of your textbook when looking at statements g and h.

   a) Acting is an exciting career.
   b) Actors and actresses / filmstars work very hard.
   c) Going to the cinema is enjoyable.
   d) Going to the theatre is boring.
   e) It is possible to learn to be an actor.
   f) Amateur/school theatre productions are fascinating.
   g) Neil's father is right.
   h) Neil should obey his father.

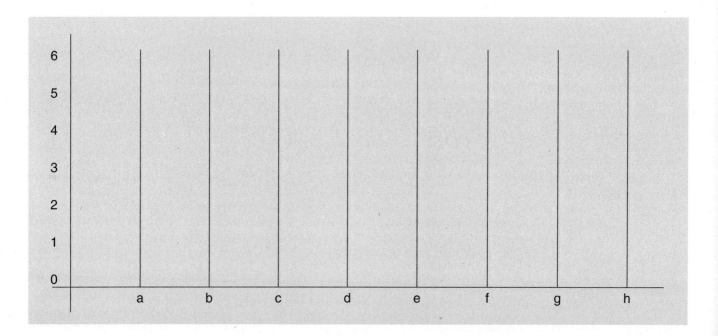

2. Compare your graph with that of a partner. Try to use the words and phrases below. (You may do this as an oral or written exercise.)

> to disagree with s.o. – to agree with s.o. – to have a different opinion to s.o. on s.th. – to have the same opinion as s.o. on s.th. – to be in agreement with s.o. on s.th.

The following qualifying adverbials will also be useful:

> much – a lot – much more/less – less – slightly – a little – fairly – very – extremely – more or less – the same as – just as

E.g. I disagree with you on this point. I think acting is a much more exciting career than you do.

6. Living dozens of great lives

1. *Collect the -ing forms in "Living dozens of great lives" on page 70 of your textbook. Explain what kind of -ing forms they are and why they are used in each case. If necessary, refer to Klett* Grundgrammatik *§ 112–123, 125–127.*

2. *Now translate lines 25–61 of the text, paying particular attention to the -ing forms.*

7. I still haven't found what I'm looking for

1. *Listen to the recording(s) of the song "I still haven't found what I'm looking for" on page 72 of your textbook. Underline any of the phrases that are close to your own reactions and opinion.*

difficult to understand	singing is of a high standard
singing is poor	will soon be forgotten
rich language	theme is trivial
will remain popular	can be interpreted in different ways
melody is catchy	too many metaphors
boring theme	same as all other rock songs
beat is catchy and imaginative	good reasons for its popularity
good sound	beat is repetitive and boring
theme is interesting and important	different harmonies

2. *Using the phrases above and then connecting words and phrases below, form sentences which support your point of view. In at least one sentence mention the recording you like better and why. You may of course include other points of your own.*

although – as – (just) because – it is (not) true that – but – and – that is why – even if – though – however – on the one hand/on the other hand – in addition – for this reason – obviously – admittedly – nevertheless

E.g. Although the sound is good I think the song will soon be forgotten.

_____
_____
_____
_____
_____
_____
_____

What is Culture Anyway?

8. What is he really like?

1. Read the poem "The Rum Tum Tugger" on page 74 of your textbook. Find the adjectives to describe the Rum Tum Tugger's character in the box (there are seventeen of them). The letters of the adjectives run from left to right and top to bottom. The first one has been given to help you.

2. Look at the line references below and decide which of the adjectives best suit them.

ll. 1, 7, ... _____

ll. 9–10, 26 _____

l. 12 _____

ll. 13–14 _____

ll. 16 _____

l. 17 _____

ll. 24, 27 _____

l. 29 _____

l. 31 _____

l. 34 _____

```
U E C C E N T R I C U H Z
N K H A Z W S T R A N G E
U O P C H I L D I S H T S
S A C L E V E R M I E K E
U R W S O Q C R P L L E L
A R Q T O D N J A A P P F
L O A U R U D E T Z F A I
Z G Y B V N L X I Y U M S
G A M B T T T R E T L O H
A N N O Y I N G N R F O V
D T I R T D W L T E D D A
B J L N R Y G R E E D Y R
A W K W A R D J S B G M F
```

3. Rewrite five of the above lines in your own words, describing the Rum Tum Tugger's character.

e.g. The Rum Tum Tugger is stubborn, because he only does what he wants to do.

Look at the following sayings and quotations which have been split in halves. Try to find the matching halves.

1. Art is long
2. The artist lives on fame
3. Every man is the architect
4. Life is a theatre
5. All the world's a stage

a) and all the men and women merely players.
b) where the worst people sometimes get the best seats.
c) but he prefers bread and cheese.
d) life is short.
e) of his own future.

And here are five more, in case you're still wondering what art is.

i) The greatest art
ii) Music
iii) Beauty
iv) Words
v) Truth

a) is in the eye of the beholder.
b) is stranger than fiction.
c) cut more than swords.
d) is the universal language.
e) is the art of life.

Now write down your ideas about art.

Answers: 1d, 2c, 3e, 4b, 5a. ie, iid, iiia, ivc, vb

5 Sensation, Information: the Media

1. Media for the masses

1. a) Look again at the song on page 76 of your textbook.
b) Close your books and share your thoughts in class on the role of the media in society. Note relevant phrases and group them in suitable ways on the board or an overhead transparency.
c) Write a paragraph about the role of the media by combining the phrases you have collected with some of the possibilities in the diagram below and the vocabulary beneath it.

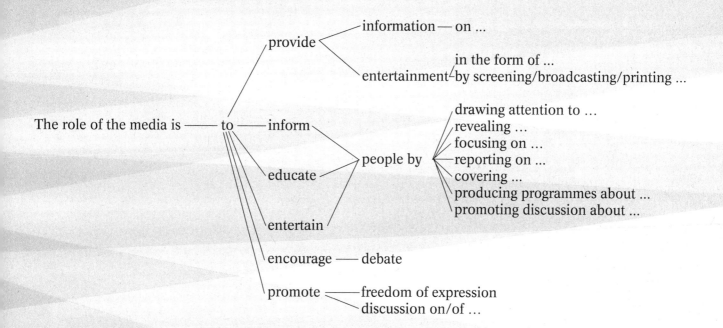

current affairs, historical events, politics, cultural and scientific developments, documentaries, topics of general interest, films, music, controversial issues, facts, articles, programmes

2. Mr Morgan and the morals of TV

1. At breakfast one day, Barbara is reading the paper and telling her partner Andrew about a letter to the editor. Complete their dialogue using tag questions, and fill in the necessary prepositions.

Barbara: Look at this! That old fellow who always moralizes – he's written another letter.

Andrew: Mr Morgan again, is it? What's he complaining about this time?

Barbara: You remember that horror film they showed .... seven o'clock the other night, _____, right when most people would be watching the box? He's complaining about what violence .... TV and videos does .... children.

Andrew: Well, it does affect them, _____?

Sensation, Information: the Media

Barbara: He's got a point, I suppose. He says it affects what they think and the way they behave .... other people.

Andrew: The trouble is, you can't prove that, _____?

Barbara: Well, he quotes some study that was done – doesn't give any names or statistics, though, so you can't rely .... that, _____? He says they've found out that if children watch violence .... the screen a lot, it will be bad .... them in the long run. It means they get used .... solving problems .... just beating people up.

Andrew: I always worry .... children having nightmares .... watching a horror film.

Barbara: That's another thing the scientists have found out, so Morgan says. They say children are frightened because they can't tell the difference .... reality and fantasy. Apparently that wrecks their nerves .... a while, and it could change their personalities.

Andrew: Those are pretty logical conclusions, _____? I mean – we don't really need scientific evidence .... think of that, _____? Why not just use our common sense?

Barbara: Sure. But still, we wouldn't be thinking .... it now if old Morgan hadn't written another letter, _____?

Andrew: Well, look who's getting moral now!

2. *The following phrases are from the letter. Match each of them with an expression in the dialogue:*

to screen a film _____

prime viewing time _____

to influence s.b. _____

attitudes _____

social behaviour _____

scientific research _____

frequently _____   long-term (effects) _____

to become aggressive _____

to be unable to differentiate between ... _____

to damage _____

3. *Now reconstruct Mr. Morgan's letter. Remember that the language would be fairly formal:*
   a) *Underline all the points in the dialogue that are quoted from the letter.*
   b) *Write the letter, using a variety of sentence beginnings. Start like this:*

   Yet again this week, a horror film was screened in prime viewing time. ...

Sensation, Information: the Media

3. Progress?

Many expressions can be translated in several ways, e.g.:

meinen	to think (so); to hold the view (that); to be of the opinion; to believe
anderer Meinung sein	to disagree, to think otherwise, to hold a different view, to think differently
Aufgrund	As a result of; Because of; Owing to; Due to

Complete the following English and German texts so that one is an accurate translation of the other, without translating word for word. Be careful of words that may be plural in one language but are always collective singular in the other (siehe Klett Grundgrammatik *§ 3–§ 5):*

A Aufgrund a)rasanter technischer Fortschritte haben wir heutzutage die b)Mittel, 1 _____ und Informationen 2 _____ c)rund um den Erdball zu senden. Nie zuvor hatten die Menschen 3 _____ so vielen Möglichkeiten, sich über die Medien d)Ratschläge zu holen und ihre Kenntnisse zu erweitern. e)Nutzen wir 4 _____ _____ aber wirklich voll aus? f)Bedeutet technischer Fortschritt, 5 _____ _____ ? 6 _____ mehr Informationen und g)Kenntnisse einen besseren Einblick und 7 _____ ? h)Wer so denkt, ist wahrscheinlich zu optimistisch. Wer aber i)anderer Meinung ist, sollte nicht die Technologie 8 _____ , sondern die Menschen, die sie 9 _____ _____ .

B As a result of a) _____ we now have the b) _____ _____ to transmit 1news and information c) _____ _____ 2within seconds. Never before have people had 3access to so many ways of d) _____ _____ and increasing their knowledge through the media. But do we really e) _____ of 4what is available? Does technological progress f) _____ 5we become more civilized? Does more information and g) _____ _____ 6mean more insight and 7understanding? h) _____ think so are probably too optimistic. Those who i) _____ , however, should 8place the blame not on the technology but on the people who 9apply it.

Sensation, Information: the Media

4. Making headlines

It is not always easy to understand newspaper headlines. The main differences between headlines and everyday speech are as follows:

A Short words are used to save space.	**POPE: NO NUKES**	The Pope has condemned nuclear weapons.
B Abbreviations stand for institutions and people in public positions.	**PM: US RELATIONS IN DANGER**	The Prime Minister has said that the relationship between Britain and the USA is in danger.
C Present simple tense refers to present or past.	**CINDY CRAWFORD AND RICHARD GERE DIVORCE**	Cindy Crawford and Richard Gere have divorced.
D *To + infinitive* expresses definite future plans.	**ULSTER PEACE TALKS TO START MONDAY**	Peace talks on Ulster will be starting on Monday.
E The past participle refers to the passive.	**ESCAPED PRISONER CAUGHT**	The prisoner who escaped recently has been caught.
F Foreign countries are usually referred to by their capital.	**WASHINGTON AND BEIJING IN TRADE WAR?**	There may be a trade war between the USA and China.

1. Look at the following sentences and try to write headlines from them. Give the letter of the appropriate rule or rules in brackets each time.

a) A man was nearly killed by a bee yesterday. _____ ( )

b) A police constable was robbed in a park last night. _____
_____ ( )

c) The Ford car company is going to build a car for singles. _____
_____ ( )

d) The British Government is planning to close several schools. _____
_____ ( )

e) A pupil beat a teacher in a game show on television. _____
_____ ( )

f) The Canadian government will soon be holding talks with the European Union on fishing rights.
_____ ( )

g) The examination results are to be announced on 1 April. _____
_____ ( )

2. Try to write a short and, if possible, humorous article for one of your headlines.

Sensation, Information: the Media

5. It's all in your hands

Is the viewer turning the TV set on or off? Give reasons for your answer.

6. "To let" or not "to let"

1. Underline each of the verbs in the following sentences that could be translated with a compound including "lassen". Write the German verb(s) at the end of the sentence.

   a) According to the advertisement in the Sunday Times many people leave their TV on during the commercial breaks, although they have left the room or do not want to watch the commercials at all.

   b) When Charles Pound, a big businessman, heard about the study showing the relative ineffectiveness of advertising on TV, he wanted to have his TV commercials stopped at once.

   c) The TV company, however, did not allow Charles Pound to go ahead with his plans because he had signed a long-term contract.

   d) The TV company kept on broadcasting the commercials and made him pay for them.

   e) Charles Pound then had his lawyers examine possible legal action.

   f) As the two quarrelling sides were not able to reach a sensible compromise, they went to court and had their case settled there.

   g) The court decided in the TV company's favour because the contract between them and Charles Pound did not allow for any other interpretation.

Sensation, Information: the Media

3. *Translate the following passage into English:*

> Nellie Nailles ließ ihren Sohn Tony viel fernsehen. Stundenlang ließ Tony die Kiste an. Er wollte den ganzen Nachmittag kein einziges Programm auslassen. Eliot Nailles war sehr verärgert über die Fernsehsucht seines Sohnes und ließ ihn das eines Tages deutlich wissen. Tony bat seinen Vater, ihn in Ruhe zu lassen. Als er die Nörgelei *(nagging)* seines Vaters nicht mehr aushielt und nach oben laufen wollte, ließ ihn Eliot Nailles sofort wieder herunterkommen. Eliot war nicht bereit, zuzulassen, daß der Junge vor dem Problem wegrannte. Nellie verließ die Küche und versuchte, mit ihrem Mann zu reden. Er ließ sich aber nicht von seiner Entscheidung abbringen: dem Fernsehkonsum seines Sohnes wollte er ein Ende setzen.

7. The missing link

Combine sentence a) with sentence b) each time by using one of the connective phrases in the box (you do not have to use them all). Replace nouns with pronouns where necessary:

| although | even though | so | in spite of / despite (the fact that) | provided (that) |
| on the one hand ... on the other (hand) | | in addition to | | unless |

1. a) A lot of people complain about the negative effects of TV.
   b) Hardly anyone ever gives up watching TV.

2. a) Scientific studies have proven beyond a doubt that advertising on TV is not very effective.
   b) Many business people still spend a lot of money on television advertising.

3. a) People use the media sensibly, i.e. selectively.   b) The media can certainly enrich people's lives.

4. a) In our multimedia world the "traditional" media – the press, radio and television – still exist.
   b) Today there are new forms of media such as computers.

5. a) My friend is an enthusiastic newspaper reader.   b) He never reads a good book.

6. a) I wanted to learn to use a computer.   b) I enrolled in a computer course.

8. Like a pioneer

Sensation, Information: the Media

1. Explain the meaning of the following words or phrases from their contexts:

   a) available at the touch of a finger _____

   b) eventually _____

   c) the technology's only in its infancy _____

   d) battery dead _____

   e) dumping addresses _____

2. *Next day, J.J. writes a letter and tells her sister about the experience — about her scepticism, her partner's enthusiasm, the irony of what happened and how her partner reacted. Complete the account.*

You wouldn't believe how mad he was the other day. He'd been at his laptop for ages – I was getting hungry because he had said he'd cook dinner that night. So I went in to see what he was doing. He said he had just _____ and exclaimed enthusiastically _____.
I couldn't quite see the point of it all. I reminded him _____
_____ and said I had thought
_____. He was convinced that
_____ and argued _____
_____. Can you believe it? More like he's the child himself, playing with his new toy! I said he _____
_____. He simply replied _____
and tried to convince me _____. I decided not to say any more and went off to make a sandwich. Next thing I heard him scream, and something hit the wall. You'll never guess what had happened: _____
_____.

39

Sensation, Information: the Media

A media quiz

1. *How many computers were there per 100 people in 1993 in each of the countries below? Fill in one of the following figures each:* 8   10   13   17   19   29

   USA ☐   France ☐   Italy ☐

   Great Britain ☐   Germany ☐   Australia ☐

   Japan ☐

2. *How many hours of television do you think the following groups in the US population watch per week?*

   a) Women 18–24 years old _____   b) Male teens _____

   c) Female teens _____   d) Men 55 and over _____

   e) Children 6–11 _____   f) Men 25–64 _____

3. *What do the following acronyms stand for?*

   BSkyB _____

   PCC _____

   CNN _____

   NBC _____

   BBC _____

4. *When did the first personal computer go on the market?*

   1965 ☐   1970 ☐   1975 ☐

5. *What percentage of working women and what percentage of working men in the USA use computers in the workplace? Circle the percentage you think is correct.*

   Women   27%   32%   43%   47%
   Men   27%   32%   43%   47%

Solutions

1. USA 29   France 13   Italy 8   GB 17   Germany 13   Australia 19   Japan 10

2. a) 25 h 42 min   b) 21 h 10 min   c) 20 h 50 min   d) 38 h 28 min   e) 19 h 59 min   f) 28 h 4 min

3. British Sky Broadcasting
   Press Complaints Commission (GB)
   Cable News Network
   National Broadcasting Company
   British Broadcasting Corporation

4. 1975 (called Altair 8800)

5. Women 43%   Men 32%

6 The UK: Continuity and Change

1. What's where?

1. Work in pairs. Partner A looks at the picture on page 42. Partner B looks at the picture on page 44. Partner A begins to describe the position of objects in his or her picture. Partner B interrupts as soon as a difference becomes obvious, e.g.:

A: There's a boat in the top left-hand corner.
B: Wait a minute – there's no boat in my picture. In the top left-hand corner there's a train.

Note ten differences in this way, using the phrases below.

| on the left – on the right | in the top left-hand (right-hand) corner | to the left/right of | above – below |
| at the bottom – at the top | in the bottom left-hand (right-hand) corner | | next to/beside |

2. Now look at map A on page 94 of your textbook. Describe what you can see around the edge of the map, using the above phrases and the vocabulary below. Look up any words you do not understand:

> furs, traders, antlers, tiger, elephant, soldier, kangaroo, Aborigine, boomerang, farmer,
> gold-digger, wool, spade, rifle, fan, to fan s.o./s.th., to lean on, to look up to, to sit at the feet of s.o.

2. A question of statistics

Work in pairs. Partner A looks at the graph on this page. Partner B looks at page 48 and describes the unemployment rate from 1965 onwards. Partner A fills in the details from the information partner B provides but does not look at partner B's page until the exercise is completed. Use the language given on page 55 of your textbook (Working with graphs). Afterwards compare your versions of the graph. What does it tell us about the UK in the 20th century?

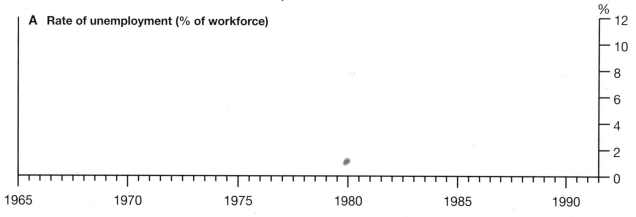

3. Test your tenses!

The text below is part of text 2 on the cassette (Additional Texts for Listening Comprehension, Klettnummer 510413). Before you listen to it again, see how many of the gaps you can fill in. Add either a verb or the correct form of the verb given. Sometimes you will also need adverbs or adverbial phrases. Check your answers by listening to the tape.

Change and continuity – a personal view

If you [1] _____ to understand Britain's changing position in the world in the 20th century I think

you [2] _____ look back to the past. A good starting point [3] _____ (to be)

those 19th-century maps of the world with large areas coloured red or pink [4] _____ (to show)

The UK: Continuity and Change

the extent of the British Empire. Maps of the world, of course, ⁵ _____ (to look) rather different today. The Empire ⁶ _____ (to go). Its loss ⁷ _____, I believe, the most dramatic change to happen to Britain in the 20th century.

Closely connected to the loss of the Empire ⁸ _____ the decline of Britain as an economic power. The colonies ¹⁰ _____ (to be) useful trading posts as well as a source of raw materials for British manufactured goods. Their loss ¹¹ _____ one reason why Britain ¹² _____ (to move) from ¹³ _____ (to be) the second most important industrial country in the world in 1870 to the 12th in 1989; in 1870 Britain ¹⁴ _____ (to have) a 45% share of manufactured exports in the world, by 1989 this ¹⁵ _____ (to fall) to as low as 9%.

Parallel to Britain's decline as a world power, its interests ¹⁶ _____ (to move) further from the Commonwealth and the USA and more towards its European neighbours. Not only ¹⁷ _____ (trade, to increase), but the British ¹⁸ _____ (also, to begin) to see Europe as more important. This ¹⁹ _____ (clearly, to show) in recent opinion polls. Britain's interest in, and integration into Europe ²⁰ _____ (no doubt, to continue, to increase) as the European Union ²¹ _____ (to develop). The Channel Tunnel, of course, ²² _____ (to help) bring Britain physically closer to Europe.

Picture for partner A, Exercise 1. What's where?

4. Justice for some

1. *Read the passage on the next page.*
2. *Imagine you are Jatinder. Use the table below the story to list what happened from his point of view and how he might have felt at each point in the story.*
3. *Comment on the way in which race relations in Britain are presented in this passage.*
   Look at page 77 of your textbook before answering. Mention the following:

   everyday problems   expectations
   role of the police   role of the community

The UK: Continuity and Change

It was still early evening when Jatinder and the others were walking home. They knew the score. One of the boy's parents ran a small corner shop – it had things like 'Paki shit' daubed on the walls. Jatinder himself got some stick when he first went to school. Not much, but enough to be painful.

Over the years they had come to accept that there would be some abuse and harassment.

They were passing a pub when several white guys came out jeering at them. Somehow it was not possible to just walk on by. Jatinder shouted something back – he could not remember later what it had been.

The white man blocked their path and told them to get off the pavement. They refused. One of the bigger men started to push Jatinder around – the friends were getting a bit worried now. The white group sensed their fear and got more aggressive. A punch was thrown – and one was returned.

It had hardly gone much further before the police were there, two vans and a patrol car. Everyone was bundled into the vans, but from the start the police seemed to assume that it was Jatinder and his friends who had started the trouble.

"You lot should all go back home," sneered one of the uniformed constables at Jatinder. "I was trying to," he mumbled under his breath.

At the station they were finger printed and shoved in a cell despite their protests that they had only been defending themselves.

By the time they were allowed to make a phone call someone who had seen the scuffle had told Jatinder's parents and Mr Ali from the community association had been to the station to protest.

Jatinder and his friends were released at 2am after the desk sergeant gave them a talking to about not getting into trouble. There seemed little point in answering back.

At the youth club a visiting community relations constable apologised to Jatinder. "If it happens again, make sure you contact me." Jatinder noted his phone number – but he never goes near the pub.

© *Commission for Racial Equality (CRE) and BBC June 1994*

2 to know the score (*informal*) to know the true facts about a situation – **4 to daub** [dɔːb] – **to get some stick** (*informal*) to be treated badly – **8 abuse** unkind, rude or cruel words and actions – **harrassment** [ˈhærəsmənt] behaviour that is meant to annoy someone – **10 to jeer** to say rude things to s.o. – **17 to throw a punch** to hit s.o. very hard with a closed hand – **27 to shove** [ʌ] (*informal*) to push – **31 scuffle** rough struggle – **35 to give s.o. a talking to** to tell s.o. how to behave properly – **38 to apologise** to say you are sorry for s.th. you have done

Event	Jatinder's feelings
Jatinda walking home	Feeling calm
Passes pub	
Constable apologises	Feels better but never wants to go to the pub again

43

The UK: Continuity and Change

5. Summer job

1. You have just written a letter of application for a summer job in Britain. Unfortunately someone tore it up by mistake. Write it out again in the correct order.

Picture for partner B, Exercise 1

> I would be most grateful if you could let me know whether you could offer me employment in the summer and if you could help me with accommodation.

> Tel +89 1234567

> Although I have never been to an English-speaking country before, I have had eight years of English at school, taught by an excellent teacher. You may be interested to know that your factory features in our textbook (*The New Skyline Edition B*). Apart from my linguistic skills I also have advanced computing skills.

> Thanking you in advance for your help and looking forward to hearing from you,

> Dr Penrose has passed on your name to me and suggested that I contact you. She informs me that you frequently offer foreign students the opportunity to work at your factory on a temporary basis. I am writing to ask you if you could offer me employment from 1 August – 15 October 1997. I enclose a full curriculum vitae and the names of two referees.

> As you can see, I finished school last summer and am about to study Business Administration at the University of Klugstadt in the southern German state of Bavaria. Before I start my studies I am keen to gain practical experience abroad.

> Application for work placement

> Dear Mr Wilcox,

> Yours sincerely,
> Roberta Hanson

> Klugstraße 1
> 80783 Klugstadt
> Germany

> 12

> March

> 1996

> Mr Victor Wilcox
> Managing Director
> J. Pringle & Sons Casting
> and General Engineering
> 2 – 5 Station Road
> Rummidge RU1 2AB
> UK

Experience the Great Outdoors

Limited opportunities exist for young Europeans (aged 18 - 21) to spend 6 months working on Australian sheep farms. Riding skills necessary. Farm experience an advantage. The chance of a lifetime to experience life in Australia! Help with travel expenses available. Apply to: Ms F. Smith, Australian Department of Employment, Education and Training, PO Box 9880, Canberra, ACT 2601, Australia

---

2. Write an application for the job advertised here. Use relevant phrases from Roberta Hanson's letter to Mr Wilcox.

6. A right Royal romp

This is an advertisement for the stage version of The Queen and I.
Do this exercise only after you have read pages 104–106 of your textbook!

1. Explain what is happening in the cartoon.
2. In the speech bubbles, write down what you think each of the characters is thinking or saying.
3. Work in groups of five. Take on the role of one of the characters above. Act out the scene in your group (from the point of the Queen's entry to a suitable conclusion that you make up yourselves), then present it to the class or to another group.
4. What does the advertisement imitate, and how does it do this? Look at pp. 82–83 of your textbook.
5. Look at the box on "cliché" on p. 138 of your textbook and the cartoon next to it. Then look at the figure of the Scotsman in this advertisement. Comment on the way he is pictured.

The UK: Continuity and Change

7 Around and about Britain

START

- Name a British rock group and say why you like them.
- Talk for 1 minute about the British Empire.
- **1930s Depression hits Britain – go back 2 spaces.**
- Name a famous British sportsman/sportswoman.
- **? Free question**
- **1973 UK joins the Common Market – go forward 2 spaces**
- **? Free question**
- What does "UK" mean?
- **1994 Ceasefire in Northern Ireland – go forward 2 spaces**
- Spell the name of the British Prime Minister.
- You have one day in London. What will you do?
- Talk for one minute about English as a world language.
- **1950s Industry booms – go forward 1 space.**
- Who is the head of the Church of England?
- Name a British novel. Tell the others about one event in it.

This is a game for two or more players. Here are the rules:

1. *Throw the dice to see who starts. Use small items (e.g. pencil sharpener) as playing pieces.*
2. *Take it in turns to throw the dice and move around the board.*
3. *In order to finish, you must have exactly the same number on the dice as you need to finish. The player who finishes first wins.*

Free Question: the other players make up a question for you to answer.

46

The UK: Continuity and Change

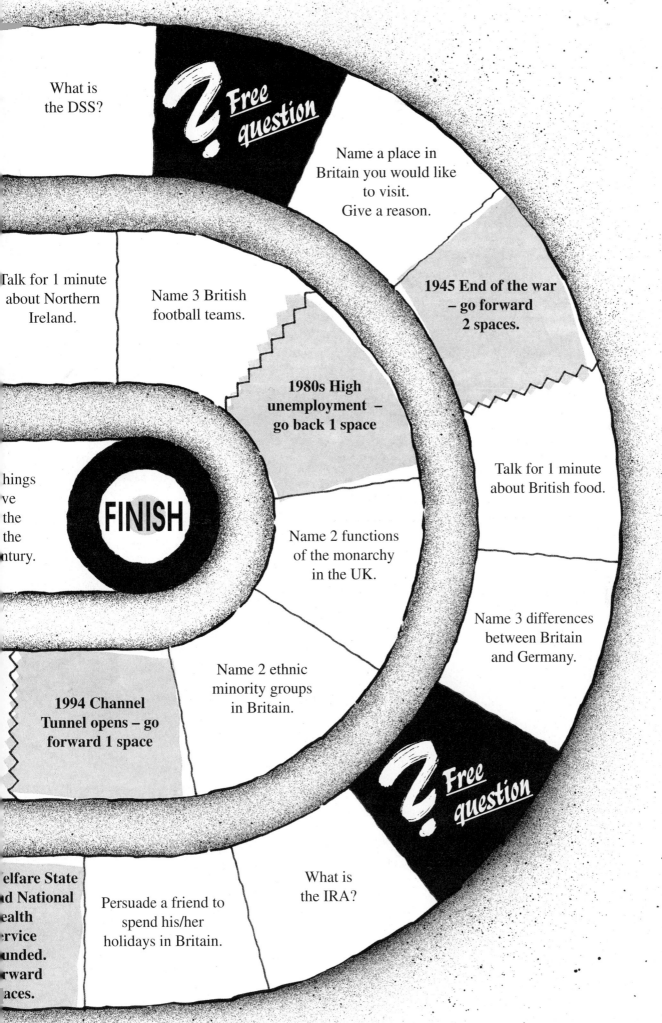

The UK: Continuity and Change

Across
1. Parliament is .... by the voters.
3. To manufacture
7. Department of .... Security
8. Followers of Britain's first woman Prime Minister
9. Britain has lost most of its enormous ....
11. 9 across has been replaced by the ....
12. Factories producing certain types of goods, e.g. textiles; described by a poet as "dark" + 13 down
14. Equal .... (chances)
15. In the 19th century Britain ruled a large part of the ....
17. Some people want to .... the monarchy.
18. The postwar period has seen the .... of Britain's manufacturing industry.
19. You work for him or her.

Down
1. West Indians are an important .... group in the UK.
2. The northern counties of Ireland
4. Ethnic .... (also: uncles and aunts)
5. Without work
6. A painful pop singer
7. Coal is found in it.
10. Britain was "the .... of the world".
11. Whitehall is the home of Britain's .... service
13. Of the devil; used to describe 19th-century factories (cf. 12 across)
16. Found below the North Sea

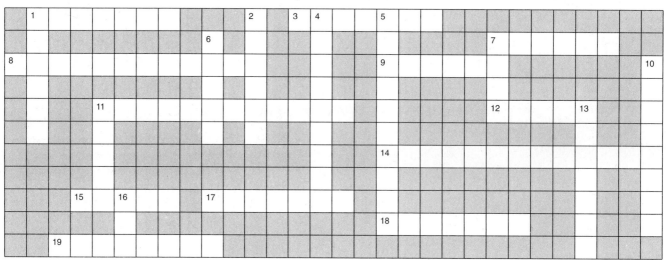

For the solution to the crossword, turn to page 64 – but not until you are finished!

Graph for partner B, Exercise 2. A question of statistics

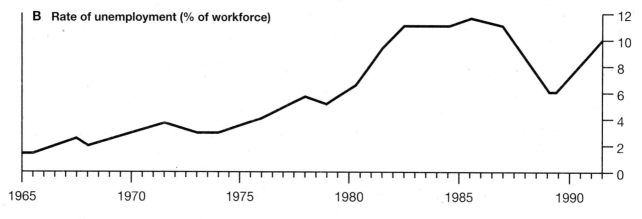

7 Enter 2000: the USA Today

1. "From California to the New York Island …"

1. Match each of the cities with the state it is located in. If you need help, look at the map on the inside back cover of your textbook.

Seattle	Michigan
Denver	Oregon
Houston	Florida
Detroit	Washington
New York	Wisconsin
Milwaukee	Colorado
Portland	Texas
San Francisco	Massachusetts
Minneapolis	Arizona
Boston	Minnesota
Orlando	New York State
Phoenix	California

2. All of the states are known by other names as well. These names tell us something about the states. The origins of the following "nicknames" are easy to work out. If some of the words are unknown to you, look them up first in a dictionary. Then finish the sentences, using the following verbs and adverbs to express certainty:

clearly – obviously – … must mean – no doubt – to imply – to indicate – to show – to refer to

a) Oregon: Beaver State *If Oregon is called the Beaver state, there must be beavers in Oregon.*

b) Florida: Sunshine State _____

c) Massachusetts: Old Colony State _____

d) Minnesota: Land of 10,000 lakes _____

3. The following names of sporting teams do not tell us immediately how they originated. With the help of a dictionary, guess what they mean, using expressions such as the following:

to sound like – might/could – to imply – perhaps – to mean – to suggest – to seem to

a) Boston Celtics (basketball): _____

b) New York Islanders (ice hockey): _____

c) Houston Rockets (basketball): _____

Enter 2000: the USA Today

    d) Detroit Pistons (basketball): _____

_____

2. It's like ....

Professor Fielding (p. 112 of your textbook) says that universities try to improve their faculties' image by hiring superstars: "They're like the Yankees buying their ball club" (ll. 103–104). We can also form comparisons using like *and an* ing*-form without a direct object ("the Yankees"), e.g.:*

    Making culture respectable in Post, Texas, was like teaching a snail to run.

1. Using ing-forms, make up endings for the following sentences, based on what Fielding says:

    a) Living in Post, Texas, must have been like _____

_____

    b) Going to the movies once a month must have felt like _____

_____

    c) Working as a traveling salesman meant _____

_____

    d) Entering Columbia University was like _____

_____

    e) Getting a life-time contract was like _____

_____

    f) Being denied tenure meant _____

_____

2. Now make up similar sentences based on your own experience, using ing-forms:

    a) Going by car in the rush hour is like _____

_____

    b) Getting a tooth out is as bad as _____

_____

    c) Failing my English exam would mean _____

_____

    d) Having the same English teacher for three years would be like _____

_____

    e) Getting up at six in the morning feels like _____

_____

3. The parable and Toni Morrison

1. Underline the phrases in the following text which tell us the level of time (past, present, etc.) the passage is operating on.
2. Fill in or complete the verbs in the correct tense, adding an adverb where given. You will also need to decide whether the verb is used actively or passively.

I wonder what Toni Morrison would say about the parable we read, "The Visit". She <u>might emphasize</u> (might, to emphasize) the way white people _benefited_ (US sp.) (to benefit) from being white in her childhood: they _were always served_ (always, to serve) in the ice-cream parlor, and they _were permitted_ (to permit) to use any part of the park they _wished_ (to wish). They _did not need_ (US") (not, to need) to be embarrassed about sitting wherever they _liked_ (to like) in the theater. They _did not know_ (not, to know) what it was like _to be repressed_ (to repress). Schools in Ohio _were integrated_ (to integrate), it's true, but society _was_ (to be) nothing like a happy melting pot. Integration _did not protect_ (not, to protect) black people from racism.

Toni remembers that her father _believed_ (to believe) blacks _were_ (to be) morally superior to whites. Imagine that while he was still alive Toni _had read_ (to read) him the parable and _had told_ (to tell) him the white students' reactions to it. How would he _have reacted_ (to react)? He would _probably have seen_ (probably, to see) the story as proof of his theory. "Anyone who _demands_ (to demand) that much money for not being white," he _might have said_ (might, to say), "_shows_ (to show) that he or she _is_ (to be) morally weak."

Toni Morrison

Enter 2000: the USA Today

4. One thing leads to another

We use the following terms to express relationships of cause and effect:

causes: because of, due to, owing to, thanks to, because, as a result of

effects: to lead to, to result in, to cause, to encourage, to produce, to contribute to, to result from, to arise from

Rearrange the following sentences using the terms in brackets. Sometimes you will need to turn the sentences around. Be careful to place adverbs in the correct position and change the type of word (e.g. adverb to adjective, adjective to noun) where necessary:

e.g. Many people become depressed and bitter **because of** repeated failure to find a job.
Repeated failure to find a job can **lead to** depression and bitterness.

1. The fear of crime leads many people to buy firearms. (because)

   Many people _____

2. Due to stress in the workplace the number of job-related illnesses is growing steadily. (to lead to)

3. Talking openly about problems often produces solutions. (to result from)

4. It is often because of poverty that people turn to petty crime. (as a result of)

5. It is not unusual for immigrants to become isolated due to the language barrier that confronts them. (to cause [them to …])

6. Some animal species are becoming extinct because pesticides are used in agriculture. (to result in)

5. How do they compare?

1. On the opposite page you will find some statistics concerning some English-speaking countries, some German-speaking countries and that Pacific power, Japan. Working in pairs, compare these countries with the help of the statistics and the phrases in brackets. Use sentence introductions such as:

   I didn't realize that … I'm surprised to learn that … Did you know that …?

   e.g. *I didn't realize that the population of the USA is almost ten times that of Canada, although the USA is a little smaller than Canada.*

Enter 2000: the USA Today

a) Size and population

CANADA
Area: 3,850,786 square miles
Population: 29,100,000

USA
Area: 3,614,165 sq.m.
Population: 260,800,000

(not quite as .../ a little smaller than)
(almost ten times)

b) Inhabitants

8,349,000   6,969,000   3,036,000
Tokyo   London   Berlin

(roughly double; more than three times)

c) Highest mountain

12,000
10,000   Fujiyama
 8,000   12,388 feet
 6,000   Zugspitze
 4,000   9,738 ft
 2,000   Ben Nevis
    0   4,419 ft

(less than half as ... as; more than three times as ... as)

d) Urbanization

Great Britain 87%   Japan 77%   USA 74%   Switzerland 60%

▨ *People living in cities*
☐ *People living outside cities*

(to a much higher degree; more/less urbanized)

e) Life expectancy (1994)

▨ Women
☐ Men

(longest; as...as)

Switzerland 82/75
USA   79/73
Japan   82/76
Germany   80/73
UK   80/74

0 10 20 30 40 50 60 70 80 90 years

2. Complete the following sentences:

a) What surprises me most is _____

_____

b) I would have thought _____

because _____

c) The reason that _____ is so high/low in _____

is possibly _____

_____

53

Enter 2000: the USA Today

I'LL NEVER FIGHT FOR WOMEN'S RIGHTS.

The Navajo is a matriarchal society. It is the Navajo woman who owns the land and the houses, and she brings to her marriage a flock of sheep that she has tended since childhood, contributions which form the basis of the couple's wealth. When Navajos meet they introduce themselves by their mother's clan name first, and then their father's, and if a Navajo woman wants her husband to go away she has only to put his saddle in front of the door and he will do just that. Navajo women have always had at least as much power and respect as Navajo men; their folk tales abound with resourceful heroines, and so do their immediate families. Generation after generation of Navajo girls are brought up guided by strong, smart women who don't raise their voices because they don't need to, and who have never had to fight for equality because they have never been without it.

AMERICAN
INDIAN
COLLEGE
FUND

*Help save a culture that could save ours
by giving to the American Indian College Fund, Dept. PN,
21 West 68th St., New York, NY 10023. 1-800-776-FUND.
We would like to give a special thanks
to US West for all their concern and support.*

Photo: Tina Begay, Tribal College Student

Enter 2000: the USA Today

6. "I'm a Native American"

1. *Look at the advertisement on the page opposite. Imagine you are going to interview Tina for your school magazine in the USA. Using the clues given below, make up questions you could ask her. Each time, use something she said in the advertisement as a starting point:*

Tina's statement	Possible question
a) matriarchal society	role of men?

   <u>You said Navajo society was a matriarchal society. What role do men play?</u>

b) girl brings flock of sheep into marriage		urban Navajo women?

   _____

   _____

c) saddle in front of door		permanent or temporary separation?

   _____

   _____

d) girls raised by women		boys' education?

   _____

   _____

2. *Imagine a sceptic reacts to the advertisement with a whole lot of doubts. Complete them using the words in brackets:*

   "It sounds too good to be true. Will this fund help you save your culture? What's the use? In a few years' time …

   a) … <u>your lifestyle will have changed completely.</u>"   (lifestyle – to change – completely)

   b) … your _____

   _____. (reservations – to become – tourist attractions)

   c) … _____

   _____. (children – lack of respect – traditions)

   d) … _____

   _____. (natural surroundings – to destroy)

   e) … _____

   _____. (money – to lack – Indian institutions)

3. *A lot of Native Americans would not be put off by such pessimism. What might they say to these challenges (a–f)? Try to think of replies Tina, the girl in the ad, might make to any three of them, e.g.:*

   Even if our lifestyle changes, we will still hold on to Navajo values.

   Use a variety of sentence structures.

Enter 2000: the USA Today

Texas!

Choose the correct answers (there may be more than one correct answer per question).

1. The origin of the name Texas is

   ☐ a) Spanish   ☒ b) Indian   ☐ c) English

2. The capital of the state is

   ☒ a) Austin   ☐ b) San Antonio   ☐ c) Houston

3. Compared in size to all other US states, Texas is

   ☐ a) no. 1   ☒ b) no. 2   ☐ c) no. 3

4. Texas is bigger than

   ☒ a) The British Isles   ☒ b) Germany   ☒ c) France

5. Texas has about

   ☐ a) 10   ☒ b) 14   ☐ c) 18 million inhabitants

6. It has more inhabitants than

   ☐ a) Scandinavia   ☐ b) Spain   ☒ c) Switzerland and Austria together

7. Texas joined the Union in

   ☐ a) 1778   ☒ b) 1845   ☐ c) 1848

8. Which of the following is NOT in Texas:

   ☐ a) the Alamo   ☐ b) Lyndon B. Johnson Space Center   ☒ c) J.F. Kennedy Library?

9. Sam Houston was

   ☐ a) a movie director   ☒ b) the President of Texas   ☐ c) an oil tycoon

10. Which American president(s) was/were born in Texas:

    ☒ a) Eisenhower   ☐ b) Clinton   ☒ c) Johnson?

Now pick the US state that interests you most and make up a similar quiz to present to your class.

Solutions
1. b) (Indian word meaning "friends")
2. a)
3. b) (Alaska is number one)
4. a) b) c)
5. b)
6. c)
7. b)
8. c)
9. b)
10. a) c)

8 Scotland: Nation or Region?

1. Scotland here I come!

You have come to Scotland for the first time. Ian, your friend in Edinburgh, is asking you what you would like to see during your three-week holiday.
*Give the answers that **you** would give, using some of the following expressions:*

I wouldn't mind	I (don't) fancy	I could imagine	I (don't) feel like	I would rather (not)
How long do you think …would take?	How about …?	I am not so keen on / not terribly interested in
Why don't we …?	Wouldn't it be better if …?	That sounds great!

Make sure your answers fit the next statement Ian makes.

Ian: You must have heard quite a lot about Scotland – Nessie and all that. And maybe some history – Mary Stuart … Would you like to see some of the famous sites here in Edinburgh?

You: _____

Ian: Well, we needn't stay in Edinburgh. The countryside is really beautiful as well, and there are some quite spectacular old castles. What about looking at some of them?

You: _____

Ian: Yes, we like walking too. We often go for long walks in the hills. Would you like to come with us?

You: _____

Ian: Oh yes. And after that we could go across to St. Andrews. Have you ever heard of the famous golf course there? It's supposed to be an extremely challenging one because it's so close to the sea and exposed to the winds.

You: _____

Ian: Well, talking about the sea, have you ever been to the islands, Skye or the Outer Hebrides? Would you fancy a trip there?

You: _____

Ian: It would take a week, at least, I guess. You don't want to arrive and take the same ferry back, do you?

You: _____

Ian: And on the way we could stop at some village. We might even come across a Highland festival.

You: _____

Scotland: Nation or Region?

Ian: Well, so far I've been firing suggestions at you. What about yourself? What else would you like to do?

You: _____

_____

Ian: That sounds interesting. Let's get something to eat now and discuss things while tasting some local specialities. How about fresh fish?

You: _____

2. Where can we stay?

1. *Look at the following list of facilities (services and equipment) available in private accommodation in Edinburgh. Look up any words you do not know in a dictionary.*

   - Credit Cards Accepted
   - Reduced Accommodation Rates for Children Under 16 Sharing Parents' Room
   - Cots available
   - Evening Meal available
   - Full Liquor Licence
   - Hairdryer for Residents' use
   - Indoor Leisure Facilities
   - Ironing Facilities
   - Most Bedrooms have Wash-hand Basins
   - Non-Smoking Establishment
   - Pay Phone for Residents' use
   - Private Car Parking
   - Pets Accepted by Arrangement
   - Residents' Lounge with TV available
   - Special Diets
   - Tea/Coffee Facility in **All** Rooms
   - Telephone in **All** Rooms
   - TV in **All** Rooms

2. *Pick the facility or facilities that would be particularly suitable for the guests named below and give a reason in each case. Vary the sentence structures as much as possible and use the following phrases where appropriate:*

   > to supply, to provide, to be/make available, to permit, to allow, (not) to mind, to be convenient, to cater for, to suit

   Draw the correct symbol in the brackets provided.

[ ] Mrs Perriwinkle and her dog   <u>Where this symbol is used, people can bring their pets with them. / Guesthouses advertising with this symbol provide facilities for pets.</u>

[ ] Mr Morton, who likes drinking tea   _____

_____

[ ] The Barnes family (children 7 and 4)   _____

_____

[ ] Julie, who hates cigarette smoke   _____

_____

[ ] Jeremy, who is allergic to dairy products   _____

_____

3. *Act out a telephone conversation, following the steps given for each partner. The steps for Partner A are given below and on the opposite page, those for Partner B on p. 60.*

Instructions for Partner A: *Partner A is yourself. You are calling the Edinburgh tourist office. Each dash represents a response from the tourist officer. Do not look at your partner or his/her notes while acting out the call! It is best to turn in opposite directions. Your notes are on the page opposite.*

Scotland: Nation or Region?

—

You: Good morning. I am looking for private accommodation in Edinburgh for two people from 5th to 12th August.

—

You: (Twin.)

—

You: (Sounds good. Price?)

—

You: (Too much.)

—

You: (Television? Make tea/coffee in room?)

—

You: (Quiet? Public transport?)

—

You: (Accept.)

—

You: (Tell details as required.)

—

You: (Thank tourist officer. End call.)

3. Glasgow has it all

1. In the brochure on Glasgow you will find several alternatives wherever an adjective is included. In each case, underline the adjective which seems most suitable to you. You may find it useful to look up some of the words in a dictionary. You should think about the meaning of the word, its usage (e.g. does it go with the noun that follows?) and stylistic value (e.g. is it formal enough?).

Glasgow
HAS IT ALL

Greater Glasgow, located on Scotland's beautiful/scenic/nice West Coast, combines the energy of one of Europe's most entertaining/busy/vibrant Cultural Capitals with the unique/unusual/varied charm of three diverse/separate/distinctive districts.

From the City of Glasgow itself, known/renowned/famous for its heritage, its different/outlying/outstanding museums and galleries and year-round/yearly/annual entertainment, to Scotland's Great Outdoors, Greater Glasgow has it all.

Be sure to explore the historic/historical Renfrew District, where both the Royal Stewart Dynasty and the Paisley pattern originated. Admire the beautiful/nice/scenic charm of Inverclyde, offering great/attractive/spectacular views over the River Clyde, or enjoy a (an) extraordinary/outstanding/superb family day out in Cumbernauld and Kilsyth District.

Booking your holiday in Greater Glasgow could not be less difficult/more comfortable/easier. Simply select the area in which you wish to stay and note your preferential/favourite/preferred accommodation. Then complete the booking form on page 24 of this guide. We will do the rest.

2. Now write a similar text in English about your town or region that could be used in a brochure advertising your area.

Scotland: Nation or Region?

4. Mary Queen of Scots

PLEASE PRINT		
Name:	Stuart, Mary	Further comments: Bothwell: suspected
Date of birth:	1542	of being Darnley's murderer
Parents:	James V of Scotland	Mary: attempts to re-establish
	+ Mary Guise	Catholicism by force
Marital status:	married	– forced to abdicate in favour of her son
Husband:	Francis II of France (1558-60)	(later James VI of Scotland) in 1567
	Lord Darnley, her cousin	– flees to England
	(1565-67)	– imprisoned there by Elizabeth I
	Earl of Bothwell (1567-71)	– beheaded in 1587 for high treason

Write an account of Mary's life, starting like this: Mary Stuart was born in 1542, the daughter of James V of Scotland and his wife Mary Guise. At the age of 16, ...

5. The place we are looking for....

1. Look at the map of Scotland on page 129 of your textbook. Choose one city or town, mountain (range), river or island, and describe its location to your neighbour. He or she has to find out the name of this place. Repeat the exercise several times, taking turns,

   e.g. *The place we are looking for is situated in the north-east, just south of the Orkneys. It is a small town. If you go there you cannot go any further north on the mainland.*

   (The correct answer is John o'Groats.)

Instructions for Partner B, p. 58
You are a tourist officer in the Edinburgh tourist office. A caller wishes to book accommodation. Reply to his/her request, referring first to advertisement A, then to advertisement B. Each dash represents a response from the caller. Do not look at the caller while acting the call.

You: Good morning, Edinburgh Tourist Office.
—
You: (Double or twin room?)
—
You: (Victorian flat, B&B, close to theatres and Castle)
—
You: (£16 per person per night)
—
You: (Another B&B, £13)
—
You: (TV yes; coffee and tea-making facilities yes)
—
You: (Reasonably quiet suburban street; close to buses)
—
You: (Ask for name, address and phone number)
—
You: (Tell caller you'll make reservation, and that the owner of the B&B will confirm booking)
—
You: (End call)

RACHEL G. ARGO
61 LOTHIAN ROAD EDINBURGH EH1 2DJ
TEL: (0131) 229 4054
Map Ref F6   Listed/Approved
Victorian first floor flat. Two minutes from Castle and Theatres.

ROOMS 1 S 1 D 1 T	OPEN 4-10
B+B per person	from £14.00 to £18.00
B+B en-suite per person	
Single price	from £14.00 to £18.00

JANIE CARTER
UPWAY 107 HILLHOUSE ROAD EDINBURGH
EH4 7AD TEL: (0131) 539 4455
Map Ref M3   Listed/Commended
Comfortable family home, convenient for airport and city centre. Friendly welcome, good bus service, parking.

ROOMS 1 S 1 T 1 F	OPEN 4-10
B+B per person	from £12.50 to £13.00
B+B en-suite per person	
Single price	from £14.00 to £15.00

Scotland: Nation or Region?

6. A tale of two characters

1. This exercise is based on the text "Sheep don't have souls" on pages 132–135 of your textbook. The old lady and her visitor do not have much in common. In fact, one can hardly imagine a greater contrast between two characters than between these two. List these contrasts.

Gentleman	**Old Lady**
a) the gentleman's lack of politeness	the old woman's respect for the stranger
b) he wishes to stay outside	

2. Now combine each pair of features in a complete sentence. Use connectives expressing the idea of contrast and opposition, e.g.

   while, whereas, but, on the one hand… on the other hand, though, although, even though, even when, yet

   e.g. *Even though the gentleman was impolite from the start, the old woman showed him the respect she showed every stranger.*

7. Lucky ladders

1. The middle term in each of the following groups of three links two phrases. With the help of the words below, find out what these phrases are. You will find clues in all the chapters of your textbook. Some terms are one word and some are hyphenated. Some usually start with capital letters.

<u>crude</u> oil <u>rig</u>	<u>crude oil</u>	<u>oil-rig</u>	
_____ mother _____	_____	_____	
_____ man _____	_____	_____	
_____ community _____	_____	_____	
_____ land _____	_____	_____	
_____ chair _____	_____	_____	
_____ time _____	_____	_____	
_____ market _____	_____	_____	
_____ union _____	_____	_____	
_____ weapons _____	_____	_____	
_____ rights _____	_____	_____	

   abuses, arm, centre, earth, economy, grand, human, ice, jack, job, kind, local, nuclear, owner, part, person, proliferation, time, trade, zone

2. Can you think of any more combinations like these? If so, see if your neighbour can guess them if given only the middle term.

Scotland: Nation or Region?

8. If only I could read your thoughts ...

1. Read the text "A grand view of the oil-rig" (in your textbook, pages 136–137) again. Look at what the crofter and his wife say to the tourists and complete the pattern:

What they say	What they are really thinking
WIFE You'll have come to see the oil-rigs – oh, they're a grand sight right enough. You'll no see them for the stour, but on a clear day you'll get a grand view if you just stand here –	WIFE *What a laugh! Ugly things, those oil rigs ...*
CROFTER Aye, you'll get a much better view now the excavators digging for the minerals have cleared away two and a half of the Five Sisters of Kintail. [...] And you'll see all the bonnie big tankers come steaming up the loch without moving from your chair – [...]	CROFTER
WIFE When the weather clears up, you'll be wanting down to the shore to see the pollution – it's a grand sight, right enough. [...] Or you can get Donnie MacKinnon to take you in his boat out to the point there, to watch the rockets whooshing off down the range –	WIFE

2. Comment on the differences between what they say and what they think.
   a) What do these tell us about the couple?
   b) How do they affect us?
   c) What may have been the playwright's aim?

3. You could act this out as follows:

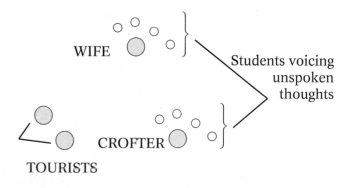

The actors speak the lines as in the text, and between segments the unspoken thoughts are heard behind them (put in as they fit).

Scotland: Nation or Region?

9. Scotland. Scotland?

1. Now that you know quite a lot about Scotland, you can do this exercise without using clichés (see page 138 of your textbook). Fill in the pattern with different items that you associate with Scotland:

	Gla	**S**	gow
		C	
		O	
		T	
		L	
		A	
		N	
		D	

2. Explain in complete sentences what your answers have to do with Scotland. Use the knowledge about Scotland that you have gained in this chapter. In other words, you should not write, "Glasgow is a city in Scotland" but "Glasgow is Scotland's largest industrial city".

10. Unique in the Western world

This exercise is based on pages 139–140 of your textbook. Fill in the correct forms of the verbs in brackets (adding should, would or must in some cases) and the adverbials. Some verbs may be in the passive voice.

P.H. Scott thought that Scotland _____ (to be) independent because it_____ (to be) under English influence for too long. He said that Scotland_____(to be) unique in the Western world because it _____(to have) its own legal system and bureaucracy but no parliament of its own. Scottish policy, he explained, _____ (always/to make) in London and thus _____ (always/to take) into account the state of the British economy more than Scottish interests. He was sure that if an economic recession _____(to strike) England, it _____ (automatically/to have) consequences for Scotland as well. Scott assumed that this _____ (to become) worse once national sovereignty _____ (partly/to transfer) to Brussels. Scott also ____ _____ (to underline) the psychological need for independence. Scots, he said, _____ (to feel) that most events of significance _____ (to happen) somewhere else. Such an attitude, Scott argued, _____ (sooner or later/to lead) to a feeling of inferiority. If something_____ (to go) wrong, he warned, Scots _____ _____ (to have) no one but themselves to blame.

Scotland: Nation or Region?

How do we get there?

In order to get from the first word to the last, you are allowed to change only one letter per line. The solutions are at the bottom of the page. More than one solution may be possible.

PINE	LIFE	FOX	GOWN	WOLF
MINE	___	___	___	___
MIND	___	___	___	___
KIND	DIME	DIG	BORN	TOLD

RIVER	STONE	HAND	WEEP	TORN
___	___	___	___	___
___	___	___	___	___
WIDEN	SWORD	___	___	___
		___	___	___
		FAIR	BEAM	SAVE

Solution to crossword on page 48

	1 E	L	E	C	T	E	D		2 U		3 P	4 R	O	5 D	U	C	E				
	T				6 S		L		E			N		N		7 S	O	C	I	A	L
8 T	H	A	T	C	H	E	R	I	T	E	S			9 E	M	P	I	R	E		10 W
	N				I		T		A					M					A		O
	I		11 C	O	M	M	O	N	W	E	A	L	T	H		12 M	I	L	L	13 S	R
	C		I				G		R			I		P					A		K
			V						O		14 O	P	P	O	R	T	U	N	I	T	I	E	S
			I						N		Y								A		H
		15 G	L	16 O	B	E		17 A	B	O	L	I	S	H					N		O
				I							E			18 D	E	C	L	I	N	E	P
	19 E	M	P	L	O	Y	E	R											C		

Solution

LIFE FOX GOWN WOLF TORN
DIVE FOG TOWN GOLF TORE
DIME DOG TORN GOLD WORE
DIG BORN WIDER DEER WAVE
WIDEN TOLD RIDER DEAR SAVE
RIVER WOLF STONE SAND DEEP WEEP TORN
STORE SWORE SAID PAID FAIR
HAND SORE SWORD PAIR BEAM
WEEP FAIR BEAM
BEAR WAVE
SAVE

64